THE
ADMINISTRATIVE PORTFOLIO

THE
ADMINISTRATIVE PORTFOLIO

A Practical Guide to Improved
Administrative Performance and Personnel Decisions

Peter Seldin
Lubin School of Business
Pace University
Pleasantville, NY

Mary Lou Higgerson
Baldwin-Wallace College
Berea, Ohio

ANKER PUBLISHING COMPANY, INC.
Bolton, Massachusetts

The Administrative Portfolio
*A Practical Guide to Improved Administrative
Performance and Personnel Decisions*

ISBN 1-882982-47-9

Composition by Deerfoot Studios
Cover design by XXX

Anker Publishing Company, Inc.
176 Ballville Road
P. O. Box 249
Bolton, MA 01740-0249 USA

www.ankerpub.com

ABOUT THE AUTHORS

Peter Seldin is Distinguished Professor of Management at Pace University, Pleasantville, New York. A behavioral scientist, educator, author, and specialist in the evaluation and development of faculty and administrative performance, he has been a consultant to more than 300 colleges and universities throughout the U.S. and in 35 countries around the world.

A well-known speaker at national and international conferences, Seldin regularly serves as a faculty leader in programs offered by the American Council on Education, the American Association for Higher Education, and AACSB International—The Association to Advance Collegiate Schools of Business.

His well-received books include: *Changing Practices in Evaluating Teaching* (1999), *The Teaching Portfolio (2nd ed.)* (1997), *Improving College Teaching* (1995, with associates), *Successful Use of Teaching Portfolios* (1993, with associates), *The Teaching Portfolio* (1991), *How Administrators Can Improve Teaching* (1990, with associates), *Evaluating and Developing Administrative Performance* (1988), *Coping With Faculty Stress* (1987, with associates), *Changing Practices in Faculty Evaluation* (1984), *Successful Faculty Evaluation Programs* (1980), *Teaching Professors to Teach* (1977), and *How Colleges Evaluate Professors* (1975).

He has contributed numerous articles on the teaching profession, student ratings, educational practice, and academic culture to such publications as *The New York Times, The Chronicle of Higher Education,* and *Change.* For his contributions to the scholarship of teaching, in 1998 he was awarded an honorary doctor of education from Columbia College (South Carolina).

Mary Lou Higgerson is Vice President for Academic Affairs and Dean of the College at Baldwin-Wallace College in Berea, Ohio. A social scientist, educator, administrator, author, and specialist in organizational communication, she has been a speaker and consultant on topics of leadership, performance counseling, conflict management, shaping mission, and leading change.

Combining her knowledge of communication literature and skills with her administrative experience, Higgerson has focused her writing, research, and consulting on the application of communication and management theory. Since 1990, she has taught a variety of topics for the American Council on Education and seminars offered through the Department Leadership Program and has served as a consultant to institutions of higher education.

She has contributed book chapters and numerous articles on the department chair as academic leader, communication skills for administrators, and issues of academic administration that have appeared in such publications as *The Chronicle of Higher Education, Journal of College and University Personnel Association, Continuing Education Review,* and *The Department Chair.* Her books include: *Communication Skills for Department Chairs* (1996), *Complexities of Higher Education Administration: Case Studies and Issues* (1993, with S. Rehwaldt), and *The Department Chair as Academic Leader* (1999, with I. Hecht as first author and W. Gmelch).

ABOUT THE CONTRIBUTORS

Cathryn Amdahl is Writing Program Coordinator at Harrisburg Area Community College in Harrisburg, Pennsylvania. Trained as a journalist, she has taught for 23 years and lives in Harrisburg with her husband, Mark, and daughter, Flannery.

Lee Bash is Dean of the Division of Lifelong Learning at Baldwin-Wallace College, Berea, Ohio. In his more than 30 years as an educator, he has enjoyed his varied roles as instructor, researcher, author, lecturer, and consultant. He has published five books, written more than 200 articles, and is a regular contributor to *Jazz Educators Journal*.

Christina DePaul is Director of the Myers School of Art at the University of Akron (Ohio). An art world pioneer in anodizing aluminum, she has lectured in the United States, Portugal, Spain, New Zealand, and Helsinki. Her work is in many collections including the White House, the American Craft Museum, and the Children's Hospital of Philadelphia.

Monica A. Devanas is Director of Faculty Development and Assessment Programs at the Rutgers University Teaching Excellence Center in New Brunswick, New Jersey. The center is responsible for both faculty development and evaluation of teaching. As director, she takes many lessons from her career in microbiology: to adapt, evolve, persist, and flourish.

Deborah DeZure is Coordinator of Faculty Programs, Center for Research on Learning and Teaching, at the University of Michigan, Ann Arbor. Previously, she served as Director of Faculty Development at Eastern Michigan University. She is a frequent presenter and has published extensively on college teaching and faculty development and evaluation.

William K. Guegold is Director of the School of Music at the University of Akron (Ohio) where he also holds the rank of professor. A past president of the Ohio Music Education Association, he was named a Distinguished

Alumnus of the Kent State University School of Music and received the 2001 Alumni Achievement Award from Capital University (Ohio).

Jane S. Halonen is Director of the School of Psychology at James Madison University in Harrisonburg, Virginia. A clinical psychologist, she has published textbooks on college success, introductory psychology, and critical thinking. The American Psychological Foundation honored her with its Distinguished Teaching Award in 2000, in part for her administrative support of high quality teaching and contributions to curriculum development in psychology.

Joyce Hickson is Chair of the Department of Counseling and Educational Leadership at Columbus State University, Columbus, Georgia. She has received the College of Education's Service Recognition Award for instructional initiatives and has been nominated for the university's 2001 Research Award.

Catherine Jarjisian is Director of the Conservatory of Music and Chair of the Music Division at Baldwin-Wallace College, Berea, Ohio. For 15 years she taught at Oberlin College where she directed the Music Education Division. She holds the Doctor of Arts in Music Education degree from Temple University.

Laurence Kaptain is Assistant Provost for Academic Affairs at the University of Missouri, Kansas City (UMKC). He focuses on organizational transformation, undergraduate curriculum and programs, and faculty development. A musician by training, he has performed internationally and recorded with the Chicago Symphony and the St. Paul Chamber Orchestra.

G. Andrew Mickley is Professor and Chair, Department of Psychology, at Baldwin-Wallace College, Berea, Ohio. Before he returned to academia, he spent 21 years as an officer and scientist in the U.S. Air Force. He is an active teacher-scholar in the area of behavioral neuroscience.

Joan DeGuire North has been Dean of the College of Professional Studies at the University of Wisconsin-Stevens Point since 1985. She was an early pioneer in the national faculty development movement. With a background in English and education, she seines through life's flotsam for treasures.

G. Roger Sell is Director of the Center for Enhancement of Teaching at the University of Northern Iowa, Cedar Falls, Iowa. His areas of concentration are faculty development, curriculum, and instructional and organizational development. He is president-elect of the Professional and Organizational Development Network (POD) in Higher Education.

John Zubizarreta is Dean of Undergraduate Studies and Professor of English at Columbia College, Columbia, South Carolina. Selected as the South Carolina Carnegie Professor of the Year in 1994, he has published and consulted widely on teaching improvement. He is also an avid telemark skier, former national whitewater canoe champion, and busy father of two daughters.

CONTENTS

PART II

Sample Administrative Portfolios

PREFACE

An important change is taking place in higher education: Academic administrators are being held accountable, as never before, for how well they do their jobs.

In the past, factual information on administrative performance has been skimpy at best. Typical administrators have been unable to present solid evidence of what they do, much less why they do it. The result: The routine approach to evaluating performance has relied almost exclusively on ratings by supervisors, perhaps supplemented by a supportive letter or two. But there is much more to administration than what is critiqued on supervisor rating forms buttressed by one or two testimonial letters.

How can administrators document superior performance or an outstanding effort to improve performance? The best way the writers know to get at both the complexity and individuality of administrative performance is the administrative portfolio.

WHAT IS AN ADMINISTRATIVE PORTFOLIO?

What is the portfolio? It is a collection of materials that document administrative effectiveness. It brings together in one place information about the scope and quality of an administrator's activities and accomplishments. It allows display of achievements for examination by others and, in the process, contributes to both more sound personnel decisions and to the professional development of individual administrators.

The Administrative Portfolio is a hands-on look at the why, what, and how of preparing and successfully using the portfolio. It offers ready-to-use, field-tested information.

Previous books on evaluating and developing administrative performance were mainly collections of administrative techniques, often focused on a specific position, such as a department chair, or academic dean. This book is different.

WHAT *THE ADMINISTRATIVE PORTFOLIO* OFFERS

- It offers practical suggestions for getting started and then maintaining the most effective use of portfolios.

- It identifies key issues, red-flag warnings, and benchmarks for success.

- It provides helpful answers to common questions.

- It carefully differentiates between portfolios for personnel decisions and portfolios for improvement in performance.

- It lists 21 possible portfolio items from which administrators can choose the ones most personally relevant.

- It includes 13 actual portfolios from across administration positions and institutions.

WHO CAN BENEFIT FROM *THE ADMINISTRATIVE PORTFOLIO*

The Administrative Portfolio is written for presidents, provosts, academic vice presidents, department chairs and program directors—the essential partners in developing successful administrative evaluation and development programs. The straightforward language, practical suggestions, and field-tested recommendations should prove valuable. The book should also be helpful to graduate students planning careers as higher education administrators.

OVERVIEW OF THE CONTENTS

The Administrative Portfolio consists of two parts. The 12 chapters in **Part One** present practical, research-based information and strategies about how to develop a good portfolio and how it can be used.

Chapter One examines the new breed of academic administrators and the need for a more open, factual, and systematic evaluation of their performance.

Chapter Two discusses the administrative portfolio concept, what it is, how it is a natural outgrowth of the widely used teaching portfolio, and why administrators might want to prepare one.

Chapter Three describes the key role of the mentor, provides practical advice on what to do and what not to do as a mentor, and discusses how to prepare a portfolio when there are no mentors available.

Chapter Four presents a seven-step approach to creating a portfolio and offers pragmatic suggestions on how to present the finished product.

Chapter Five examines the wide range of items that might be included in a portfolio, differentiates between documenting outcomes (results) and behaviors (activities), discusses how to integrate them, and shows how to select appropriate appendix items.

Chapter Six outlines in important detail (including different tables of contents) how to use portfolios for personnel decisions (evaluation) and how to use them to improve performance. Specific guidelines for developing a successful administrative portfolio program are also included.

Chapter Seven offers pragmatic answers to questions commonly raised about developing and using portfolios. Here is a discussion of how the portfolio differs from the usual end-of-the-year report. The chapter also addresses why all portfolios don't look alike, how much time it takes to produce one, why portfolio mentors and models are so important, why an impressive looking portfolio cannot gloss over poor administrative performance, and why the time and energy required to prepare a portfolio are worth the benefits.

Chapter Eight describes the step-by-step development of an administrative portfolio, including determining the purpose for creating one, identifying potential readers, developing the table of contents, choosing a mentor, selecting specific items, and organizing the appendices.

Chapter Nine examines the proactive role of the mentor and describes how the mentor's approach to working with the administrator helps to shape both the process of portfolio development and the final product.

Chapter Ten discusses how to implement an administrative portfolio review program that simultaneously responds to the need for performance evaluation, facilitates performance improvement, sustains professional development, and strengthens the institution.

Chapter Eleven discusses in a question-and-answer format such issues as the value of writing a portfolio if the administrator is the only person who reads it, there is no campus requirement to do one, or the administrator does not plan to change jobs.

Chapter Twelve is a personal report by the former director of the Faculty Center for Instructional Excellence, Eastern Michigan University, on her portfolio preparation, how she looked critically at her own administrative performance, what she found out, and why she is a strong advocate of the portfolio.

Part Two of *The Administrative Portfolio* contains the 13 actual portfolios that have been developed and used by administrators in different positions and in different institutions across the country. These 13 documents demonstrate application of the advice and strategies presented in Part One and are rich sources of ideas.

Peter Seldin
Pleasantville, New York
August 2001

Mary Lou Higgerson
Berea, Ohio
August 2001

PART I

The Administrative Portfolio: Purpose, Process, and Product

1

CHANGING ROLES AND EXPECTATIONS OF ACADEMIC ADMINISTRATORS

A dministrators today face a series of unrelenting demands. The work pace has quickened, budgets are tight, collegiality has been replaced by a we-versus-they mentality. Today's academic administrator is expected to know how to handle fiscal and budgetary matters; to be able to deal with trustees, government agencies, and courts; and to be an expert in public relations, fundraising, and collective bargaining. The administrator is also expected to excel in human relations, budget analysis, organizational strategy, and managerial skills. In short, the job of the academic administrator has become more complex, more pressured, more businesslike.

At the same time, government agencies are imposing restrictive rules and regulations on administrators in higher education. So are accrediting groups and funding agencies. Computers are producing dramatic changes in the way things are done. The demand for accountability has become a groundswell across the nation, and it has forced institutions to assess the productivity and examine the cost effectiveness of each department and each program, as well as the individual performance of each academic administrator.

Unfortunately, factual information on administrative performance is at best often skimpy. Typical academic administrators have little factual information about what they do, why they do it that way, or how well they do it. True, they probably have a list of programs they've developed and perhaps some letters of invitation or thanks. But a list of programs plus some letters fall far short of a complete picture of one's administrative effectiveness. They may have a curriculum vitae, but typically that says very little about their administrative performance. Yet in the absence of factual information about what they do, why they do it that way, and how well they do so, it is very difficult to evaluate their performance. It is also very difficult to reward it. And it is very difficult to improve it.

Informal evaluation of administrative performance has long been practiced in academic institutions. Much of it is the result of casual observation. Faculty members pick up impressions of an administrator's competence and swap these impressions with their colleagues. Students form opinions about administrative effectiveness after encounters with them. Even administrators gain fragmentary impressions about fellow administrators and give voice to their impressions. In short, a campus has many individuals who harbor casual opinions about the quality of the work of others.

What is new, however, is the attempt to root out hearsay and gossip in favor of more open, factual, and systematic evaluation of administrative performance.

Is there a way for academic administrators to respond simultaneously to the movement to take academic administration seriously and to the pressures to improve systems of administrative accountability? The answer is yes. A solution can be found by turning to the administrative portfolio, an adaptation of the teaching portfolio.

2

THE ADMINISTRATIVE
PORTFOLIO

What is an administrative portfolio? It is a collection of materials that document administrative performance. It brings together in one place information about the scope and quality of an administrator's activities and accomplishments. It allows display of administrative achievements for examination by others and, in the process, contributes to both sounder personnel decisions and to the professional development of individual administrators (Seldin & DeZure, 1999).

It is important to point out that the administrative portfolio is not an exhaustive compilation of all the documents and materials that bear on administrative performance. Instead, it presents selected information on administrative activities along with solid evidence of their effectiveness. Just as in a curriculum vitae, all claims made in the portfolio must be supported by firm empirical evidence.

Why would very busy—even harried—administrators want to take the time and trouble to prepare an administrative portfolio? They might do so in order to gather and present hard evidence and specific data about administrative effectiveness for those who judge performance. Or they might do so in order to provide the needed structure for self-reflection about which areas of their administrative performance require improvement.

There are other purposes for which administrators might prepare a portfolio. Seldin (2000) says they might do so in order to a) seek administrative awards, grants, or merit pay; b) leave a written legacy within their administrative unit so that future generations of administrators who will take over their positions will have the benefit of their thinking and experience; c) share their experience and expertise with other administrators; d) prepare materials about their administrative effectiveness when applying for a new position; or e) document for themselves how their administrative style has evolved over time.

Some may argue that busy administrators should not spend their valuable time preparing a portfolio. Seldin (2001) offers this answer: As administrators, he says, we regularly update our curriculum vitae. But those vitae merely contain skeleton outlines of what we do. They don't get at the issues of how we do it or why we do it in a particular way. And just as important, the curriculum vitae doesn't possess the special power that portfolios do to engage administrators in reflecting on their own policies and practices and how to improve them.

The logic behind portfolios is straightforward. Earlier evaluation methods, such as evidence of impact on college/university committees, were like flashlights. That is, they illuminated only those administrative skills and abilities that fell within their beams. As such, they shed light on only a small part of an administrator's performance. But with the portfolio, the flashlight is replaced by a searchlight; its far broader beam discloses the broad range of administrative philosophy, attitudes, abilities, and skills.

Edgerton, Hutchings, and Quinlin (1991) and Smith (1995) make the case for teaching portfolios that are also readily adaptable to administrative portfolios:

1) Portfolios capture the individuality and complexity of academic administration. They offer meaningful evidence which can provide the foundation for reflection, discussion, and evaluation. And portfolios are grounded in the specifics and contexts of a particular administrative position in a particular college or university at a particular point in time.

2) Portfolios place the responsibility for evaluating administrative performance with the administrator. Evaluation is not something that is done *to* administrators. Rather, it is something done *with* them. The initiative is placed in the hands of the administrator who selects, assembles, and explains portfolio entries that represent actual performance.

3) Portfolios prompt reflective practice and improvement. In the preparation of the portfolio, the administrator is forced to ponder personal administrative activities, organize priorities, rethink administrative strategies, and plan for the future. Portfolios display the thoughts behind the action, not just the results.

4) Portfolios can foster a culture of administrative professionalism. Because portfolios are best prepared in consultation with others, they involve interaction and mentoring and, as a result, are a step toward a more public view of academic administration.

REFERENCES

Edgerton, R., Hutchings, P., & Quinlin, K. (1991). *The teaching portfolio: Capturing the scholarship in teaching.* Washington, DC: American Association for Higher Education.

Seldin, P. (2000). *The teaching portfolio.* Paper presented for the American Council on Education, Department Chair Seminar, Tampa, FL.

Seldin, P. (2001). *The administrative portfolio.* Paper presented for the American Association for Higher Education, National Conference. Washington: DC.

Seldin, P., & DeZure, D. (1999). *The administrative portfolio: An adaptation of the teaching portfolio.* Paper presented for the American Association for Higher Education, National Conference, Washington, DC.

Smith, R. A. (1995). Creating a culture of teaching through the teaching portfolio. *Journal on Excellence in College Teaching, 6* (1), 75-99.

3

THE IMPORTANCE OF
COLLABORATION

Portfolios can be prepared by the administrator working alone. But this isolated approach has limited prospects for improving performance or contributing to personnel decisions. Why? Because portfolios prepared by the administrator working alone do not include the collegial or supervisory support needed in a program of improvement. And, importantly, there is none of the control or corroboration of evidence that is essential to sustain personnel decisions. From mounting experience, we know that portfolio development should involve interaction and mentoring in the same way that a doctoral dissertation reflects both the efforts of the candidate and the advice of the mentor.

Zubizarreta (2001) points out that collaboration balances the administrator's subjectivity with objective criteria. It ensures a fresh, critical perspective that encourages cohesion between the portfolio narrative and supporting appendix evidence. Millis (1995, p. 70) describes her view of mentoring in connection with teaching portfolio development, a view that is readily adaptable to administrative portfolio development:

> The mentor's role is to help shape reflections, to encourage discovery and create meaning. . . . To respect the integrity of the person, the process, and the final product, I refrain from imposing my own assumptions, purpose, form, or style . . . I always ask what their expectations are for my role and how much direct assistance they desire. Their preferences are respected. My mentoring role is that of a guide, not a director.

Since administration tends to be a private, solitary activity, collaboratively designed portfolios are an antidote to isolation and a way to promote collegial exchange.

Who might serve as a mentor? An administrator's immediate boss might do so. But more often the mentor is another administrator either at the same institution or at another one in the same geographic area. For example, within the same institution, a department chair in history might mentor a chair in sociology. Or an academic vice president might mentor an academic dean. Similar mentoring arrangements might be made between administrators across institutions.

The mentor discusses with the administrator such guiding questions as: Which areas of the administrative process are to be examined? What kinds of information do they expect to collect? How will the information be gathered? How will it be presented? Why are they preparing the portfolio? (This is especially important because the purpose drives the content and organization.)

To be effective, the mentor must have wide knowledge of procedures and current instruments to document effective administrative performance. But having such content knowledge alone is no guarantee of effective mentoring. To truly be effective, the mentor must also have the interpersonal skills and attitudes necessary to develop the relationship needed for mentoring.

SELF-MENTORING

Although the authors strongly recommend that portfolios be developed collaboratively, they are keenly aware that sometimes there are no willing and able mentors available. In that case, even though the important collaborative aspects of portfolio development will be lost, it is still possible to prepare a portfolio. Here are some self-assessment questions that may help:

- Does the portfolio clearly identify your administrative responsibilities?

- Does the reflective statement adequately and accurately describe your administrative philosophy? strategies? methodologies? objectives?

- Does the portfolio reflect consistency between your reflective statement and your administrative actions?

- Is every claim made in the narrative supported by hard evidence in the appendices?

- Is the degree of documentation between information from yourself and information from others in general balance?

- Is the vast majority of data current or from the recent past?

- Does your portfolio contain performance evaluation data from multiple sources? Possible sources include your supervisor, faculty, peers, students, the people who report to you.

- Does it contain evidence of impact on areas of your responsibility?

- Have you included information on efforts to improve/develop your administrative performance?

DISCUSSION WITH THE ADMINISTRATOR'S SUPERVISOR

Whether the portfolio is prepared by the administrator working with a mentor or working alone, discussion should occur between the administrator and the person he or she reports to in order to address expectations and how administrative performance is to be reported. Otherwise, there is a danger that the supervisor may erroneously conclude that the data submitted overlooks areas of prime concern and may even cover up areas of suspected weakness. Such possible misunderstanding is largely eliminated by open discussion, perhaps accompanied by an exchange of clarifying memos. This is especially important when the portfolio is prepared for personnel decisions.

REFERENCES

Millis, B. (1995). Shaping the reflective portfolio: A philosophical look at the mentoring role. *Journal on Excellence in College Teaching, 6* (1), 65-73.
Zubizarreta, J. (2001). Private discussion.

4

STEPS TO CREATING AN ADMINISTRATIVE PORTFOLIO

E xperience suggests that most administrators rely on the following sequence of steps to create their portfolios. This is based on the teaching portfolio work of Shore and others (1986), Rodriguez-Farrar (1995), Seldin (1997), and Seldin and DeZure (1999), and is readily adaptable to administrative portfolios.

1. Introduction
The administrative portfolio typically begins with an introduction which describes the purpose of the portfolio (improvement? personnel decision? grant? seek employment?), the institutional context (size, mission, public or private), and the administrative unit directed by the administrator (department? college? institution?). Its overall length is usually no more than three or four paragraphs.

2. Summarize Administrative Responsibilities
This statement of responsibilities covers such items as supervision of others; participation on institutional committees, task forces, and planning groups; budget supervision; dissemination of materials; service to faculty or students; programs or services. It also includes any agreement, formal or informal, between the administrator and the person to whom he or she reports concerning specific administrative responsibilities. Its length rarely exceeds one page.

3. Describe Your Approach to Administration
Bearing in mind the summary of responsibilities described in Step 2, the administrator prepares a two- to three-page reflective statement describing his or her philosophy, strategies, methodologies, and objectives. The statement addresses the issue of *how* the administrator carries out responsibilities

from the standpoint of *why* they do what they do. It also provides specific examples of administrative practices which show how the individual's methodologies fit their goals and the institutional context.

4. Select Items for the Portfolio

From the list of possible items for a portfolio, the administrator selects those which are most applicable to his or her administrative responsibilities and approach to handling them. A factual statement about describing accomplishments in each area is then prepared. The items chosen for the portfolio reflect the administrator's personal preferences, administrative style, and particular responsibilities. Being creative and inclusive in itemizing accomplishments and offering reflections on them builds a personalized portfolio.

5. Prepare Statements on Each Item

Statements are prepared by the administrator on activities, initiatives, and accomplishments on each item. Backup documentation and appendices are referenced, as appropriate. Among key questions that might be considered: Do you have measures of your administrative effectiveness? Have you participated in workshops or seminars (such as the American Council on Education two-day leadership development program for academic vice presidents, provosts, and chairs designed to improve effectiveness?) Have you identified your five most significant accomplishments? Have you received administrative awards or recognition?

6. Arrange the Items in Order

The sequence of the statements of accomplishment in each area is determined by their intended use. For example, if the administrator wishes to demonstrate enhanced administrative problem solving ability, entries that reflect that goal (such as participating in the International Association for Management Education New Deans Seminar) would be stressed.

7. Compile the Supporting Data

Supportive evidence for items referred to in the portfolio should be retained by the administrator. Included might be such things as performance evaluation data from varied sources, evidence of impact on areas of responsibility, letters of invitation or thanks, administrative recognition, evaluations from programs organized and/or presented by the administrator. Such evidence is backup material and is placed in the appendix or made available upon request.

8. Present the Portfolio

Experience suggests that it is best to present all of the portfolio in a unified container, typically a single three-ring binder. Secure and flexible, the binder encourages the efficient arrangement of documents and materials in separate sections labeled with identification tabs.

REFERENCES

Rodriguez-Farrar, H. B. (1995). *Teaching portfolio handbook.* Providence, RI: Center for the Advancement of College Teaching, Brown University.

Shore, M. B., et al. (1986). *The teaching dossier,* (revised ed.). Montreal: Canadian Association of University Teachers.

Seldin, P. (1997). *The teaching portfolio: A practical guide to improved performance and promotion/tenure decisions,* (2nd ed.). Bolton, MA: Anker.

Seldin, P., & DeZure, D. (1999). *The administrative portfolio: An adaptation of the teaching portfolio.* Paper presented for the American Association for Higher Education, National Conference, Washington, DC.

5

CHOOSING ITEMS
FOR THE PORTFOLIO

In deciding what to include in the portfolio, it is important to consider whether the focus should be on outcomes (results) or behaviors (activities).

OUTCOMES AND BEHAVIORS

Most administrative portfolios concentrate on behaviors, such as decision-making, planning, organizing, and communicating. One reason for this is that administrative outcomes are hard to identify. Another reason is that the outcomes can be confused and contaminated by outside factors that the administrator cannot control. By comparison, the behaviors of administrators are relatively free of contaminates and more easily identified and evaluated.

However, there is an undeniable advantage to the inclusion of some outcome data in the portfolio. The spotlight is on results, and in the minds of many, nothing equals the importance of results.

There are advantages and disadvantages, then, in orienting the portfolio either to outcomes or to behaviors. Each can be appropriate and each can offer valuable insight into administrative performance. For that reason, many administrators include both results and activities in their portfolios.

What qualities and activities might be included? A review of the literature indicates that they often include knowledge and capacity, dependability, adaptability, interpersonal relations, commitment to professional growth, resource and personnel management, institutional loyalty, flexibility, knowledge about position, and judgment.

PERFORMANCE EVALUATION DATA

One thing is sure: A key ingredient in virtually all portfolios is performance evaluation data. Just as it is best to use multiple sources of data in evaluating faculty teaching performance, it is best to use multiple sources of data in evaluating administrative performance.

Whose performance evaluation data should be included in the administrative portfolio? Certainly, the immediate supervisor is the mainstay of performance evaluation data. But while many supervisors are excellent sources of data, prudence suggests that evaluation data in the portfolio be broadened to include additional raters so that the performance judgment rests on a wide base.

This isn't difficult and, in truth, many institutions already use a combination of sources. An Illinois college, for example, evaluates its department chairs by collecting data from the academic dean, faculty, staff, peers, and a sampling of students. A California university evaluates the faculty development director on the basis of data obtained from faculty, university administrators, staff, and the faculty development board of advisors.

Different administrative positions cater to different types of documentation. For example, an academic vice president is far removed from the director of the writing center. A faculty development specialist is worlds apart from the director of graduate studies. The items chosen for the portfolio depend on 1) the purpose for which the portfolio is being prepared, 2) the institutional context of the administrative position, 3) the importance assigned by the administrator to different items, and 4) any content requirements of the administrator's institution. Differences in portfolio content and organization should be encouraged to the extent they are allowed by the institution.

Since the portfolio is a highly personalized product, like a fingerprint, no two are exactly alike. Some administrators address an item at length while others address the same item with just a sentence or two, or even omit it.

The following is not an inclusive list. Rather, it suggests the many possibilities from which an administrator can select items relevant to his or her particular situation.

MATERIAL FROM ONESELF

- An introduction describing the purpose of the portfolio, the institutional context, and the administrative unit directed by the administrator

- A statement of administrative responsibilities, including supervision of others, budget, programs, services, grants, recruitment, curriculum development, participation on committees

- A reflective statement by the administrator describing personal administrative philosophy, strategies and objectives, methodologies

- A description of steps taken to evaluate and improve one's administrative skills/behaviors, including changes resulting from self-evaluation; time spent reading books or journals; participation in seminars, workshops, and professional meetings

- A self-evaluation by the administrator including a personal assessment as well as an explanation of any contradictory or unclear documents or materials in the portfolio

- Contributions to, or editing of, a professional journal on administration, such as *The Department Chair: A Resource for Academic Administrators* or *Academic Leader*

- A personal statement describing administrative goals for the next three to five years, along with a time frame for accomplishing each

- A list of workshops/services/programs offered or organized by the administrator

- Evidence of help given to colleagues leading to improvement in their professional performance

- The five most significant administrative accomplishments

- A record of colleagues, graduate students, or interns who have been mentored—formally or informally—by the administrator

- Evidence of needs assessment of students, faculty, or other administrators

- Evidence of impact on teaching effectiveness, staff development, or institutional improvement

MATERIAL FROM OTHERS

- Multisource performance evaluation data from individuals or groups capable of assessing administrative performance. Possibilities are the administrator's immediate supervisor, peers in the institution, faculty members, those who report to the administrator, subordinates, students, clients served. Evaluation data might cover such areas as planning, decision-making, ability to deal with people, communication skills, problem solving, resource management

- Evidence of impact on areas of responsibility. Examples: annual reports, participation levels in programs you have organized, testimonials, letters of appreciation, records (for example, change in number of department faculty, budget growth)

- Administrative awards or recognition (local, regional, statewide, national)

- Statements from others who have worked directly with the administrator in such areas as programs, services, committees, budget, recruitment, curriculum, student advising, policy determination, teaching improvement

- Documentation of on- or off-campus administrative development activity

- A statement by the administrator's supervisor assessing his or her contribution to the administrative unit and/or to the institution's mission and culture

- An audio or videotape of the administrator chairing a committee, working with students or faculty or other administrators

- Invitations from outside organizations to present a paper at a conference on academic administration (such as the Society for College and University Planning) or write a journal article on academic administration for a publication (such as *AGB Reports,* published by the Association of Governing Boards)

- Invitations to other colleges or universities to discuss effective administrative methods, or to participate in administrative symposia

- Participation in local, regional, state, or national activities related to academic administration

THE APPENDIX

The appendix material needs careful attention to be sure all the statements of accomplishment in the narrative are adequately supported. It's best not to engage in overkill.

The appendices must be of manageable size if they are to be read. Millis (1995) suggests that teaching portfolios be organized around two directives—integrity and lucidity—that are readily adaptable to administrative portfolios. By integrity, she means that certain key items, such as performance evaluation data and evidence of impact on areas of responsibility, are expected and must be included to support the validity of the portfolio. Further, says Millis, a key test of the lucidity of the appendices is if they are clear to potential readers, especially those outside of the administrative area; for example, a college dean reading the portfolio of a history department chair.

Many administrators weave references to appendices within unified essays rather than offer a separate isolated commentary for each appendix item. Why? Because this approach strengthens coherence. It permits the integration of materials from the administrator as well as materials from others. As a result, it offers a coherent administrative profile in that all parts support the whole. For example, a statement of philosophy might reflect a chair's emphasis on letting faculty members know what's expected of them while feedback from department faculty members would provide their assessment on the matter.

Another example: With regard to the portfolio item, "evidence of impact on areas of responsibility," a faculty developer might include data showing increasing levels of participation in programs and services, while testimonial letters from participants would attest to the impact of such programs and services on their teaching.

A word of caution: The appendices—the supporting documents and materials—should not determine the portfolio creation. The tail doesn't wag the dog. Seldin and DeZure (1999) suggest that a far better approach is to first reflect about one's philosophy of administration, then describe the strategies and methodologies that flow from that philosophy (why you do what you do) and only then to select documents and materials which provide hard evidence of one's administrative activities and accomplishments.

HOW LONG IS THE TYPICAL PORTFOLIO?

The typical administrative portfolio has a narrative of approximately eight to 12 double-spaced pages followed by a series of appendices that provide documentation for the claims made in the narrative. Just as information in the narrative should be selective, so should the appendices consist of judiciously chosen evidence. Materials should be carefully sorted to support the narrative.

Being selective does not mean creating a biased picture of one's administrative performance, but rather providing a fair and accurate representation of it. Though he was writing about teaching portfolios, Zubizarreta (1994, p. 324) makes a point that is readily adaptable to administrative portfolios: "Even the occasional flop is worthy material for a . . . portfolio if it reveals a process of genuine adjustment and growth."

If the appendices contain nonprint media or items that do not fit within the portfolio three-ring binder—such as videotapes or diskettes—the administrator may briefly discuss the materials in the narrative and make them available for inspection in a designated location.

Some institutions put a ceiling on the number of pages or number of pounds they permit in order to prevent data overkill in the portfolio.

HOW MUCH TIME DOES IT TAKE
TO PREPARE THE PORTFOLIO?

It depends. If the administrator currently prepares an annual report, he or she probably already has a good deal of the material on hand. For example, they probably have a list of their administrative responsibilities, data on performance evaluation, information on developmental workshops or seminars they have attended, letters of invitation or thanks. When they have that information on hand, preparation of the portfolio will probably take between 12 and 15 hours, spread over a number of days.

But if the administrator does not currently do an annual report, the needed documents and material are likely to be scattered and less organized. In that case, it probably will take between 15 and 20 hours, spread over a number of days, to put together the portfolio.

Whether the administrator has an annual report or not, a large part of the preparation time is spent in thinking, planning, gathering, and sifting the documentation.

As preparation of the portfolio becomes routine and administrators gain experience and skills, portfolios win an accepted place in institutional life. Administrators generally appear willing to invest time and energy in an evaluation process over which they have some control. If they know that their administrative portfolios will be carefully scrutinized by their superior or by others, it stands to reason that they will take greater pains to routinely collect materials and develop their portfolios.

THE VALUE OF SELF-REFLECTION

Self-reflection is one of the most valuable parts of the administrative portfolio. Serious, thoughtful, self-reflection can help administrators uncover new discoveries about themselves.

Seldin and DeZure (1999) suggest that the following topics may assist in the process of self-reflection: How do you work with faculty (or chairs or deans) who are struggling in their jobs? How do you work with students who are academically struggling? What new administrative strategies have you tried in the last year? How successful were they? What did you learn from the success (or failure) of those new approaches? Which parts of your administrative position do you handle most (or least) effectively? Why? What have you learned about yourself as an administrator that needs changing this year?

REFERENCES

Millis, B. (1995). Shaping the reflective portfolio: A philosophical look at the mentoring role. *Journal on Excellence in College Teaching, 6* (1), 65-73.

Seldin, P., & DeZure, D. (1999). *The administrative portfolio: An adaptation of the teaching portfolio.* Paper presented for the American Association for Higher Education, National Conference, Washington, DC.

Zubizarreta, J. (1994, December). Teaching portfolios and the beginning teacher. *Phi Delta Kappan,* December 1994: 323-326.

6

USES OF THE PORTFOLIO

Administrative portfolios are prepared for different reasons. Among others, say Seldin and DeZure (1999), they include the following:

- Administrators nearing retirement are preparing portfolios in order to leave a written legacy so that those administrators who will be taking over the position will have the benefit of their experience.

- Graduate students are preparing portfolios to bolster their credentials as they enter the job market.

- Portfolios are being prepared by administrators seeking a different administrative position, either within their institution or at a different college or university.

- Portfolios are being used to help determine winners of outstanding administration awards or for merit pay consideration.

- Colleges and universities are requesting portfolios from finalists for administrative positions (such as director of faculty development, department chair, division head, academic dean, even academic vice president).

- Administrators are also preparing portfolios so that they can provide data on their performance to persons and organizations operating off campus, such as government agencies, boards of trustees, alumni, the general public, advocacy groups.

But Seldin points out that most portfolios are prepared for personnel decisions or administrative improvement.

Using the Portfolio for Personnel Decisions (Evaluation)

To provide a rational and equitable basis for personnel decisions (evaluation) is a central reason for preparing an administrative portfolio. Such decisions have always been made by colleges and universities, but the circumstances surrounding them are changing.

In the present climate of mandatory accountability, the annual review of faculty, student evaluations of teachers, and peer evaluations of research, administrative performance needs to be evaluated in a systematic way. As Eble (1978, p. 122) cautioned in a prescient observation: "Serving purely at the pleasure of the administrative hierarchy and being subject to no more scrutiny than the offhand one of a higher-ranking administrator are ill-advised practices."

Today, many colleges and universities agree with that perspective and, as a result, they are looking toward portfolios as a more appropriate way to assess administrative performance. These institutions have concluded that personnel decisions (evaluation) should rest on a holistic examination of the administrator's performance. The focus should be not on a single stone but rather on the mosaic formed by all of the stones.

Some argue that administrators should be given unrestricted freedom to select the items that best reflect their performance. That approach works well if the portfolio is developed for improvement.

But it doesn't work well if the portfolio is developed for personnel purposes (evaluation). Why? Because the contents are based on a combination of availability of supporting materials; the nature of the portfolio; the administrative position; and the strategies, objectives, and methodologies of the individual administrator. The resulting lack of standardization makes comparability across portfolios virtually impossible.

One answer is to require portfolios being used for personnel decisions or for administrative awards or recognition to include certain mandated items along with the elective ones. Such mandated items might include, for example, a reflective statement describing 1) administrative philosophy, strategies, methodologies; 2) innovations and assessment of their effectiveness; 3) performance evaluation data which suggest an overall rating of effectiveness/satisfaction. All additional items included in the portfolio would be selected by individual administrators.

Administrators stand to benefit by providing their portfolios to evaluators of their performance. It provides evaluators with evidence upon which to make judgments about their effectiveness. If certain items in the portfolio are standardized, comparison of administrative performance (four finalists competing for the position of academic dean, for example) becomes possible.

Does the administrative portfolio really make any difference? Consider these typical comments from administrators whose portfolios were used for purposes of personnel decisions (evaluation).

A department chair: "I have no doubt that the portfolio led to my award as department chair of the year at this university. It told the selection committee what I do, how I do it, and why I do it that way."

A director of faculty development: "The portfolio was instrumental in my getting this job. It gave the evaluation committee a clear sense of my priorities, values, and strategies."

A department chair: "I knew I was an effective department chair. But now others do, too. That's why I was sent to the Harvard University Management Development Program for promising academic administrators."

An academic dean: "There were three finalists for the position of associate dean here. Their portfolios gave both the evaluation committee and me the kind of in-depth information we needed to make the right choice."

A table of contents identifies the major headings of the portfolio. A typical table of contents in a portfolio prepared for personnel decision (evaluation) might include the following entries:

ADMINISTRATIVE PORTFOLIO
Administrator's Name
Unit/Department/College
Institution
Date

Table of Contents
1) Introduction
2) Administrative Responsibilities
3) Statement of Administrative Philosophy
4) Administrative Methods, Strategies, Objectives
5) Multisource Performance Evaluation Data
6) Evidence of Impact on Areas on Responsibility
7) Five Most Significant Administrative Accomplishments
8) Administrative Awards, Recognition
9) Statement by the Administrator's Supervisor Assessing the Administrator's Contribution
10) Contributions to Administrative Conferences / Journals / Books
11) Administrative Goals: Short-Term and Long-Term
12) Appendices

Using the Portfolio to Improve Performance
The contemporary academic administrator deals with a bewildering array of tasks and issues. He or she is expected to perform as a master manager of financial, physical, and human resources, and to display the skill of a surgeon, the wisdom of Solomon, and the strategy of a field general.

The core problem, of course, is that most administrators have not received training in the skills demanded of them. For that reason, just about every college and university administrator is in need, in one or more areas, of professional and personal development and job improvement. It may be the need to update personnel policies, legal issues, planning, or budget, or it may be the need to sharpen personal skills and operating strategies in connection with leadership, time and stress management, communications, and delegation. It may be the need for personal renewal.

There is no better reason to prepare a portfolio than to improve performance. The process of thoughtful reflection augmented by the gathering and integrating of documents and materials on performance provides data with which to assist the faltering, to motivate the tired, to encourage the indecisive.

Administrators are hired by institutions in expectation of first-class performance. To help administrators hone their performance is nothing more than a logical extension of this expectation. Improvement becomes possible when the administrator is confronted with portfolio data showing strengths and weaknesses—data that the administrator accepts as fair and accurate. Preparation of a portfolio can thus serve as a springboard for performance improvement.

It is in the very process of creating the collection of documents and materials that comprise the portfolio that the administrator is stimulated to 1) reconsider policies and activities; 2) rethink strategies and methodology; 3) revise priorities, and 4) plan for the future.

The portfolio is an especially effective tool for improvement of performance because it is grounded in a specific administrative position (such as faculty developer, department chair, or academic dean) at a particular institution at a particular time.

When used for improvement purposes, the portfolio contains no mandated items. Instead it contains only items chosen by the administrator. For example, the administrator may decide to improve one particular aspect of his or her administrative performance and include such items as 1) a summary of administrative methods used; 2) specific objectives and the degree of achievement of those objectives; 3) a description of steps taken to improve performance; 4) administrative innovations and assessment of their effectiveness; 5) an audio or videotape of the administrator chairing a committee, working with students or faculty or other administrators.

A portfolio written for improvement may focus less on material from others, and more on reflective analysis, action planning, and self-assessment. But materials from others are still important, especially if the administrator can incorporate the benefits of detailed, written reviews of performance into comprehensive and specific strategies for improvement (Seldin, 2001).

Whether improvement actually takes place depends on the kind of information that turns up in the portfolio. It won't be successful unless the administrative elements to be strengthened are specifically singled out. If the portfolio is to stimulate improvement in administrative performance, it must have multiple items and the data must be detailed, thoughtful, and diagnostic. Do portfolios actually improve performance? The answer is yes, but not always. Experience suggests that if the administrator is motivated to improve, and knows how to improve, or where to go for help, improvement is quite likely.

Consider these comments:

An academic vice president: "If this concept had been around 20 years ago, I would have been a more effective department chair and a more effective dean."

A department chair: "In truth, I was skeptical. But the portfolio really helped me sharpen my administrative goals and strategies."

A faculty developer: All faculty developers—new or experienced—can improve their performance by preparing a portfolio. It forces you to directly confront the issue of why you do what you do."

A division head: "All nine chairs in this division have now completed their administrative portfolios. Some griped, of course. But in the end, every one of the nine agreed that the benefits were well worth the time they invested to put it together."

What would the table of contents look like in a portfolio for improvement? It might include the following entries:

ADMINISTRATIVE PORTFOLIO
Administrator's Name
Unit/Department/College
Date

Table of Contents

1) Introduction
2) Statement of Administrative Responsibilities
3) Administrative Methodology, Strategy, Objectives
4) Description of Steps Taken to Evaluate and Improve Administrative Skills and Behaviors
5) Documentation of On- or Off-Campus Administrative Development Activity
6) An Audio or Videotape of the Administrator Chairing a Committee, Working with Students or Faculty or other Administrators
7) Self-Evaluation Focusing Specifically on What's Gone Well, What Hasn't, and Why
8) Administrative Innovations and a Candid Assessment of their Effectiveness
9) Multisource Performance Evaluation Data Suggesting Strengths and Areas of Needed Improvement
10) Administrative Goals: Short- and Long-Term
11) Appendices

Guidelines for Developing a Successful
Administrative Portfolio Program
The following guidelines, suggested by Seldin (2001), can be helpful in developing and maintaining a successful administrative portfolio program:

1) The program must be presented in a candid, complete, and clear way to every academic administrator. Each individual must know the requirements and evidence needed for evaluating their performance.
2) Administrators must have a significant hand in both the development and the operation of the portfolio program. They must sense that they are in control of their destiny. The advantage of getting them to participate actively in the development of the portfolio program is that they will own the program and will more readily accept its implementation.
3) The primary purpose of the portfolio program should be to improve the quality of the administration, and its approach should be positive rather than punitive.

4) Top-level administrators must give their active support to the idea of administrative portfolios as a vehicle to evaluate performance for purposes of personnel decisions (evaluation) and for improvement. They must be publicly committed to the program and willing to provide whatever resources are needed.

5) All administrators must know the performance standards by which their portfolios will be judged. Specifically, they must know what constitutes exemplary, satisfactory, and unsatisfactory performance.

6) Room must be allowed for individual differences in portfolios, so long as those differences can be tolerated by the institution. Styles of administration differ. So do administrative responsibilities. The documents and materials in the portfolio of a department chair will be somewhat different from those of a director of a teaching and learning center.

7) The portfolio must provide reliable and valid data at the proper technical level.

8) The portfolio program must be firmly rooted in the purposes and academic culture of the particular college or university. Policies and procedures that work well in one institution may falter or fail in another.

9) To survive, the portfolio program must be accepted by those who prepare them. Individuals who do not endorse the system, or do so reluctantly, are unlikely to spend the time and effort to develop their portfolios in a thoughtful and meaningful way.

10) The portfolio program must recognize the responsibilities and obligations of each administrator and any special circumstances or conditions in effect when he or she was hired.

11) Performance evaluation data from only a single source, such as the administrator's immediate superior, must be discouraged. Far better is to include multisource information from superiors, those who report to the administrator, faculty, students, alumni, administrative peers, and the administrator him or herself.

12) Even if the goals of the administrative portfolio program are pure and honorable, not everyone will embrace it. Some opponents argue that the sheer diversity of administrative roles makes any portfolio system unworkable. Others scoff at the portfolio technique as unproven. But counterarguments to these objections are a) flexibility can be introduced into the portfolio process to offset diversity, and b) literally scores of colleges and universities have successfully used the portfolio approach.

REFERENCES

Eble, K. (1978). *The art of administration: A guide for academic administrators.* San Francisco, CA: Jossey-Bass.

Edgerton, R., Hutchings, P., & Quinlin, K. (1991). *The teaching portfolio: Capturing the scholarship in teaching.* Washington, DC: American Association for Higher Education.

Higgerson, M. L. (1996). *Communication skills for department chairs.* Bolton, MA: Anker.

Millis, B. (1995). Shaping the reflective portfolio: A philosophical look at the mentoring role. *Journal on Excellence in College Teaching, 6*(1), 65-73.

Rodriguez-Farrar, H. B. (1995). *Teaching portfolio handbook.* Providence, RI: Center for the Advancement of College Teaching, Brown University.

Seldin, P. (1997). *The teaching portfolio: A practical guide to improved performance and promotion/tenure decisions,* (2nd ed.). Bolton, MA: Anker.

Seldin, P., & DeZure, D. (1999). *The administrative portfolio: An adaptation of the teaching portfolio.* Paper presented for the American Association for Higher Education, National Conference, Washington, DC.

Seldin, P. (2000). *The teaching portfolio.* Paper presented for the American Council on Education, Department Chair Seminar, Tampa, FL.

Seldin, P. (2001). *The administrative portfolio.* Paper presented for the American Association for Higher Education, National Conference. Washington: DC.

Shore, M. B., et al. (1986). *The teaching dossier,* (revised ed.) Montreal: Canadian Association of University Teachers.

Smith, R. A. (1995). Creating a culture of teaching through the teaching portfolio. *Journal on Excellence in College Teaching, 6*(1), 75-99.

Zubizarreta, J. (1994, December). Teaching portfolios and the beginning teacher. *Phi Delta Kappan,* December 1994: 323-326.

Zubizarreta, J. (2001). Private discussion

7

ANSWERS TO COMMON QUESTIONS ABOUT THE ADMINISTRATIVE PORTFOLIO

In recent years, the writers have discussed the administrative portfolio concept at different colleges and universities. They have also presented papers on it at several national conferences. In the course of this activity, certain questions were raised by administrators or professors with much greater frequency than others. This chapter is devoted to answering those questions.

1. How does the administrative portfolio differ from the usual end-of-the-year report to an immediate superior?
First, the portfolio empowers administrators to include documents and materials that, in their judgment, best reflect the breadth and depth of their performance. It is not limited just to items posed by their immediate superiors. Second, the portfolio is not prepared by the administrator in isolation, but rather is based on collaboration and mentoring. Third, the purpose of the portfolio determines what is included and how it is arranged. Fourth, the process of portfolio preparation often stimulates administrators to reflect on why they do what they do. For many, this reflection results in improved administrative performance.

2. Don't all portfolios look alike?
Not at all. In truth, the portfolio is a highly personalized product, and no two are exactly alike. Both the content and organization vary widely from one portfolio to another. Varying importance is assigned by different administrators to different items. (See the sample portfolios, this volume.) Different administrative positions cater to different types of documentation. For example, the position of psychology department chair at a small

liberal arts college is worlds apart from that of graduate school dean at a large university. And the position of director of an academic division at a large community college is far removed from that of vice president for academic affairs, even at the same institution.

3. How long is the typical portfolio?

The typical portfolio has a narrative of approximately eight to 12 double-spaced pages, followed by a series of appendices that provide documentation for the claims made in the narrative. Just as information in the narrative should be selective, so should the appendices consist of judiciously chosen evidence.

If the appendices contain nonprint media or items which do not fit within the portfolio cover—such as supplemental descriptions, diskettes, videotapes, or audiotapes—the administrator may briefly discuss these materials in the narrative and make them available for inspection in a designated location.

4. How much time does it take to prepare a portfolio?

It depends. If the administrator currently prepares an annual report, he or she probably already has a good deal of material on hand. In that case, preparation of the portfolio will probably take between 12 and 15 hours, spread over a number of days. But if the administrator does not currently do an annual report, the needed documents and materials are likely to be scattered and less organized. In that case, it probably will take between 15 and 20 hours, spread over a number of days, to put the portfolio together.

5. Who owns the portfolio?

The portfolio is owned by the administrator. Decisions about what goes into the portfolio are generally cooperative decisions between the administrator and mentor. But the final decision on what to include, its ultimate use, and retention of the final product, all rest with the administrator.

6. How does a portfolio offer a coherent administrative profile?

A sound administrative portfolio integrates material from the administrator and from others. All parts support the whole. For example, not only will the statement of administrative philosophy reflect an administrator's emphasis on continuous improvement, but comments from peers and one's immediate supervisor will, too. Another example: The statement of strategies and methodologies will indicate the use of an open door policy, while performance evaluation data from faculty members and those who report to the administrator will bolster that claim.

7. Can an impressive portfolio gloss over weak administrative performance?

That's a contradiction in terms because the weak administrator cannot document effective administrative performance. The evidence is just not there. Supporting material must be provided for every claim made. For example, an administrator who claims that an immediate supervisor evaluation rates his or her performance as outstanding must provide rating forms that bear out this statement in the appendix. An elegant portfolio cover and fancy typeface cannot disguise weak administrative performance, any more than it can for a student. On the other hand, for an excellent administrator, the portfolio offers an unmatched opportunity to document administrative practices that have previously gone unrecognized and unrewarded.

8. Why are portfolio mentors and models so important to administrators who are preparing their own portfolios?

Most administrators come to the portfolio process with no prior experience with the concept. That's why the resources of a mentor are so important. The mentor—who is similar to a dissertation advisor—provides resources, makes suggestions, and offers steady support during the portfolio's development. In the same way, models enable administrators to see how others—in different administrative positions—have combined documents and materials into a cohesive whole.

9. Since the role of the mentor is so crucial to the portfolio's objectivity, how are mentors recruited?

Once administrators have been taught about the portfolio and coached by trained mentors from outside the institution, a core group of administrators emerges as experienced leaders who can help others in developing their portfolios. How can they do so? By sponsoring in-house workshops, by helping administrators connect with mentors, and by setting up a library of reading materials and sample portfolios.

10. Doesn't the subjectivity of the portfolio interfere with its use for personnel decisions or improvement of performance?

Surprisingly, it doesn't because of the collaborative effort between an administrator and a mentor who helps steer the portfolio toward meeting the needs of improvement or assessment. Portfolios prepared by the administrator working with a mentor include the collegial or supervisory support needed in a program of administrative improvement. And, importantly, there is the control and corroboration of evidence that is essential to sustain personnel decisions. Collaboration ensures a critical perspective that encourages the necessary cohesion between the portfolio's narrative and appendices.

11. Should all evidence in the portfolio be explained?

The answer is yes. Why? Because unexplained evidence is difficult for readers to understand and interpret. For example, including statements from the administrator's immediate supervisor assessing his or her contribution to the administrative unit in different years provides evidence of administrative change over time. But the significance of the change and why it took place are not apparent. That is why the addition of a commentary explaining why specific changes were made provides more convincing evidence about the administrator's efforts to improve performance.

12. How can administrators demonstrate continuous efforts to improve their performance?

They can document and explain recent administrative innovations and the reasons for those innovations. They can also describe the positive impact of professional development activities (workshops, conferences) on their administrative performance. The following list suggests the kinds of evidence that might be included.

- Detailing changes in administrative performance that resulted from careful analysis of performance evaluations

- Attending or participating in professional development workshops or conferences focused on administrative behaviors, strategies, or values and detailing what was learned, how it was applied, and how it impacted administrative performance

- Describing innovative administrative practices and the reasons for introducing those practices

- Providing two videotapes (from different years) of the administrator chairing a committee and describing changes in leadership style

- Providing two descriptions (from different years) of the five most significant administrative accomplishments and suggesting reasons for the changes over time

13. Should the mentor be from the same administrative level as the person who is preparing the portfolio?

The process of collaboration is not position-specific. For that reason, it is not necessary that a department chair, for example, be mentored by another department chair or that an academic dean be mentored by another academic dean. In fact, it is often advantageous for the mentor not to know the details of the administrative position from personal experience. In that way, the mentor can more readily concentrate on assisting the administrator to document effectiveness instead of focusing on how the administrator handles a particular aspect of his or her job (such as delegating tasks to others).

14. How would you suggest encouraging resistant administrators to prepare portfolios?

Some administrators automatically resist portfolio development. They say they are not comfortable as self- promoters, don't need to develop defensive documentation, or have neither the time nor the desire to keep a record of their achievements. But these arguments can be disposed of by pointing out that this is an age of accountability, and administrators a) need positive documentation to support accomplishments, b) must produce better evidence of contributions, and c) need to convey those accomplishments and contributions clearly and persuasively to others for inspection.

15. What guidelines would you suggest for getting started with portfolios?

To say that the administrative portfolio approach is useful is one thing, but to get the approach off the ground is quite another.

If the portfolio approach is ultimately to be embraced, an institutional climate of acceptance must first be created. How can that be done? The following guidelines should be helpful:

- Obtain top-level administrative support (the president or academic vice president) for the portfolio concept and an institutional commitment to provide the necessary resources to launch the program successfully.

- Start small.

- Involve the institution's most respected administrators from the beginning.

- Rely on administrative volunteers, and don't force anyone to participate.

- Field-test the portfolio process.

- Keep everyone fully informed about what is going on every step of the way.

- Allow sufficient time—a year or even two years—for acceptance and implementation.

16. How often should the portfolio be updated?

Most administrators do so every year. Updating the portfolio demands no more than keeping files of everything related to administrative performance, in the same way that files are kept of everything relating to a professor's research or publication.

17. Are the time and energy required to prepare and maintain a portfolio really worth the benefits?

In our view, and in the view of virtually every administrator we've mentored, the answer is a resounding yes. It usually takes no more than a few days to prepare the portfolio, and the benefits are considerable. What are those benefits? The portfolio provides an opportunity for administrators to describe their professional strengths and accomplishments for the record, a clear advantage for personnel decisions. But the portfolio does more than that. Many administrators find that the process of portfolio development itself is a stimulus to self-improvement. And many colleges and universities are finding portfolios a useful means to underscore administrative effectiveness as an institutional priority.

8

BUILDING THE
ADMINISTRATIVE PORTFOLIO

In the preceding chapters, the writers describe what an administrative portfolio is, why and how it can be useful, and delineate the basic ingredients required to create one. This chapter details the process of building an administrative portfolio.

STEP 1. DETERMINE THE PURPOSE FOR BUILDING AN ADMINISTRATIVE PORTFOLIO

The task of building an administrative portfolio will progress more smoothly if the administrator begins by reflecting on the purpose and audience for the portfolio. Why compile a portfolio? Will it serve as a means to evaluate and improve performance in the administrator's current position? Will it be used as part of a formal performance appraisal? Will the portfolio to be used to seek another position? Is the administrator preparing the portfolio to leave a written legacy to benefit others who will assume similar responsibilities? The administrator may intend for the portfolio to serve multiple purposes, but it will be important to distinguish between the primary and secondary purposes because the priorities for building a portfolio are likely to influence decisions about its content.

STEP 2. IDENTIFY THE ANTICIPATED READERS OF THE PORTFOLIO

Once the purpose for preparing a portfolio is clear in the administrator's mind, it should be relatively easy to identify the anticipated readers (self? supervisor? prospective employer? review committee? search committee?). The list of anticipated readers will inform decisions about how best to structure and draft the portfolio narrative. For example, if the sole purpose is self-reflection to further improve job performance, the administrator can abbreviate the explanation of position responsibilities that would be needed if the portfolio were to be read by someone who is less familiar with the administrator's current responsibilities. If the portfolio will be used to support a job application, the content needs to include description sufficient for readers who have no familiarity with the administrator's current position and duties. It will be useful to keep the anticipated readers in mind as the administrator moves through the portfolio building process and makes decisions about its content.

STEP 3. DEVELOP THE TABLE OF CONTENTS FOR THE ADMINISTRATIVE PORTFOLIO

It is helpful to develop the overall plan for the portfolio before the administrator begins to write. In Chapter Six of this text, the writers provide some suggestions on what the table of contents might look like for an administrative portfolio compiled for the purpose of evaluation, and how the table of contents might be altered to prepare a portfolio for improvement. The administrator is not bound to use either of these models. Rather, the specific table of contents included in the administrative portfolio should be unique to the administrator and the purpose for building the portfolio. For example, if the administrator is building a portfolio for improvement but also wants the reflective process inherent in portfolio writing to help assess the best job fit, the administrator may want to add a section that details those aspects of the administrator's current position which are enjoyable and comfortable and those which the administrator finds extremely uncomfortable to perform. Conceptualize the table of contents as a road map that directs the reader in discovering who the administrator is and why the administrator functions as he or she does in the position.

STEP 4. WRITE THE BASIC PORTFOLIO INFORMATION

The portfolio should include certain basic information even though the actual presentation of this information will vary from one portfolio to another. The administrator's portfolio should include an introduction, a summary of administrative responsibilities, and a description of the administrator's approach to administration. These three components typically become the first three sections of the portfolio.

The introduction describes the purpose of the portfolio (improvement? personnel decisions? grant? seek employment? legacy?), the institutional context (size, mission, campus culture, public or private), and the administrative unit directed by the administrator (department? division? college? institution?). The overall length of the introduction is usually no more than three or four paragraphs.

The summary of administrative responsibilities should read like an operational position description. It should be more than a list of what the administrator does in that the statement of administrative responsibilities should provide a sense of the breadth and complexity of the administrator's current duties. For example, rather than merely listing a task force that the administrator chairs, offer a brief description of the responsibility that allows the reader to assess the magnitude of the activity (e.g., chair campus-wide task force appointed by the president). Similarly, if the administrator spends a significant amount of time nurturing untenured faculty, describe the magnitude of this responsibility by giving the number of untenured faculty currently mentored and providing specific examples that illustrate the type of professional coaching offered.

It is helpful to organize the summary of administrative responsibilities so that the reader can easily grasp the magnitude and complexity of each administrative duty. If, for example, the bulk of the administrator's time is spent on personnel matters because the administrator chairs a department of 40 full-time and dozens of part-time faculty, then the personnel responsibilities of the administrator's position should be listed first. If during recent years a significant portion of the administrator's time has been directed toward fundraising and development activities, give this responsibility a more prominent placement in the summary statement.

Do not limit the administrator's summary to tasks included on the generic position description included in the institution's policy manual if the assigned responsibilities have changed or expanded beyond those listed. Typically individuals who are very skilled at their job take on more responsibilities than the duties listed in initial position description. One advantage of preparing an administrative portfolio is to illustrate how a particular position has evolved to encompass new responsibilities. The summary should also include any agreement, formal or informal, that the administrator may have made with the supervisor concerning specific and/or additional responsibilities that the administrator has undertaken. The summary of administrative responsibilities rarely exceeds one page in length.

The third item of basic information included in all administrative portfolios is a description of the administrator's approach to administration. In the table of contents, the administrator may wish to title this statement, "philosophy of administration," "approach to administration," "administrative objectives and methodology," or "administrative strategies." Whatever the specific title, this statement is a two- to three-page reflective description of the administrator's perspective on how one should carry out the responsibilities of the position. In this section, the administrator informs the reader about how and why the administrator carries out the assigned responsibilities as he or she does.

The statement will have more meaning if the administrator includes specific examples of administrative practices that show how the methodologies used fit administrative objectives within the context of the institution's mission and campus culture. In this section, the administrator provides the reader with a sense of the values and priorities that the administrator brings to the position and the administrator's logic for decision-making, approach to supervising others, and manner for working with colleagues. This section of the portfolio offers the reader a more insightful look at how the administrator does the job than the reader might get from observing the administrator. When assessments are based on third-party observations, the administrator being described or evaluated is at the mercy of those things the observer elects to notice, whereas the administrator controls the content of the portfolio and, therefore, builds the perceptual frame from which the reader will view and assess the administrator's performance. At a minimum, make certain that the portfolio addresses the key aspects of how the administrator approaches the position responsibilities.

STEP 5. SELECT A PORTFOLIO MENTOR

The writers recommend that the administrator use a mentor in building the portfolio. In Chapter Three of this text, the authors describe the benefits of collaboration and suggest who might serve as a mentor for the portfolio process. Depending on the purpose for preparing the portfolio, the ideal mentor may be the administrator's supervisor or another colleague at the home institution. The administrator may also use a professional colleague from a different institution. The mentor can be anyone the administrator believes can coach him or her through a reflective process in which the administrator analyzes how he or she performs administrative responsibilities. To be effective, the mentor must have the interpersonal skills and attitude necessary to develop the type of relationship needed for effective mentoring. The administrator's mentor must also have knowledge of measures and procedures for assessing effective administrative performance.

The administrator will want to select and involve the mentor after determining the portfolio purpose and anticipated readers. If the administrator's mentor is unfamiliar with the portfolio, the mentor may find it helpful to review this text before beginning work. Once the mentor is briefed on the portfolio, he or she will be ready to review the draft introduction, summary of administrative responsibilities, and statement of administrative philosophy. If the administrator finds it difficult to draft these items, he or she will want to involve the mentor to talk through the content of the first three sections of basic portfolio information.

Please remember that the administrator's mentor can only be effective in helping prepare the portfolio if the administrator engages openly in a reflective collaboration about his or her administrative responsibilities and job performance. The administrator must resolve to approach this exercise in an objective, analytical manner. If he or she becomes defensive, there is not much that the mentor can do to help, and the administrator will fail to realize the many benefits of preparing an administrative portfolio.

If, for any reason, the administrator decides to self-mentor, the writers recommend that he or she read Chapter Nine on serving as a portfolio mentor and answer the questions recommended for mentors. The administrator should consider using a colleague to discuss one or more specific issues relevant to the portfolio to help with the decisions that are best made when corroborated. For example, if the administrator is unsure whether a particular illustration evidences a certain skill, the administrator can corroborate the thinking on this one aspect with someone even if the administrator does not have a mentor for the entire portfolio writing process.

STEP 6. SELECT ITEMS FOR THE PORTFOLIO

In addition to the basic portfolio information (introduction, summary of responsibilities, and description of administrative philosophy), the administrator will want to select other items that illustrate his or her administrative style (behaviors) and offer evidence of administrative effectiveness (outcomes). The items that project the style will describe how the administrator approaches such activities as decision-making, planning, organizing, and communicating. The items that indicate the administrator's effectiveness will inevitably include demonstrable results (awarded accreditation, grants received, increased diversity) and performance evaluation data. The items included in the portfolio should provide the reader with an assessment of the administrator's capacity for, and effectiveness in, performing the assigned responsibilities. Collectively, the items included in the portfolio should give the reader a clear impression of such important aspects as the administrator's knowledge about the position, acumen for resource and personnel management, interpersonal skill, professional judgment, and commitment to professional growth.

The items included in the portfolio may come from oneself or from others. In Chapter Five of this text, the writers present a sampling of the types of items that might be included in a portfolio. While this is not an exhaustive list, it illustrates the range of items that might be selected to evidence the administrative style and effectiveness. It is important to remember that no single item in the portfolio can possibly provide a comprehensive view of the administrator's performance. Rather, the reader's impression of that performance will culminate from a summative review of all the items included in the portfolio. The selection of particular items for the portfolio offers comment on the administrator's personal priorities and preferences, administrative style, and particular responsibilities.

Since the portfolio derives from a reflective, collaborative process, it is possible that each new step will cause the administrator to fine tune previous steps. For example, as the administrator chooses the items to be included in the portfolio, he or she may find it necessary to modify the table of contents or to retitle some of the sections of the portfolio. The administrator may even want to reconsider the purpose for building a portfolio and perhaps sharpen the focus of the introduction to the portfolio.

STEP 7. PREPARE STATEMENTS ON EACH ITEM

For each of the administrative responsibilities listed, prepare a statement of the administrator's activities, initiatives, and accomplishments. If, for example, one responsibility is faculty development, the administrator may engage in such activities and initiatives as conducting annual performance counseling sessions with individual faculty, starting a mentoring program for new faculty hires, or implementing a teaching portfolio program focused on improvement of individual faculty. The administrator's accomplishments might include coaching six untenured faculty through successful tenure application and securing funds from the central administration to support faculty travel to professional conferences. The objective for the statement is to inform the reader of the nature and extent of work performed by the administrator for each position responsibility.

STEP 8. SELECT AND ORGANIZE THE APPENDICES

The narrative of the typical portfolio is approximately eight to 12 double-spaced pages. The items included in the narrative are supported by documentation that is presented in a series of appendices. Resist the temptation to include many lengthy documents as appendices. The appendices will only serve the intended purpose if they are of a manageable number and length for the reader to digest. The information presented in the appendices serves as supportive evidence for statements made in the portfolio. Documents presented as appendices may include performance evaluation data, reports, letters from accrediting bodies or other external reviewers, and documents or materials prepared by the administrator in performing assigned responsibilities.

The administrator may find it useful to flag the statements made in the draft portfolio that warrant some type of supporting evidence and make certain that there is appropriate and sufficient support for each statement included in the appendices. It is entirely possible that one supporting item can be used to document several statements. For example, if one major responsibility involved preparing a department for accreditation review, the letter from the accrediting agency is likely to address many, if not all, of the varied aspects of this administrative responsibility.

STEP 9. PRESENT THE PORTFOLIO

It is efficient and practical to organize the portfolio in a single three-ring binder that arranges the various documents and materials in separate sections labeled with identification tabs. Once everything is in final form, the administrator will want to allow his or her portfolio mentor to review it. If the administrator has collaborated with a mentor in building the portfolio, the administrator will discover that the mentor is as invested in the final product as the administrator. Consequently, portfolio mentors are typically excellent proofreaders.

If possible, the administrator may want to have the portfolio reviewed by one or a few individuals who did not collaborate on its preparation to determine if the portfolio achieves the intended purpose. The writers recommend that the administrator meet individually with anyone reading the portfolio to hear firsthand the reader's reaction to it. The session will be more productive if the administrator resists the temptation to defend what is in the portfolio but asks specific follow-up questions in order to understand how the content was received. Such invited reviews of the portfolio will provide the administrator with useful feedback on whether the portfolio content and presentation serves the intended purpose.

9

SERVING AS AN ADMINISTRATIVE PORTFOLIO MENTOR

The mentor plays a critical role in helping to shape the content and presentation of the administrative portfolio by providing the collegial or supervisory support essential to a program of improvement. While portfolios can be prepared by the administrator working alone, experience dictates that the preferred method is to involve a mentor who will collaborate with the administrator throughout the portfolio building process.

The mentor's role is proactive and not passive in that the mentor serves as colleague, coach, and confidant to the administrator. In doing so, the mentor balances the administrator's inherent subjectivity. For many administrators, the process of working with a mentor to prepare an administrative portfolio is the first experience with purposeful reflection about the job. It may also be the first time that the administrator has articulated the assumptions and logic that motivate his or her administrative style and performance. Consequently, the mentor's approach to working with the administrator helps to shape both the process and the product. In this chapter the writers detail the responsibilities of the portfolio mentor.

TASK 1. FAMILIARIZE YOURSELF WITH THE ADMINISTRATOR'S CURRENT ROLE AND RESPONSIBILITIES

The mentor must have a working understanding of the administrator's current position. It is not safe or wise to assume that positions with similar titles are the same from one campus to another or even from one department to another at the same institution. Such important factors as department size, discipline, and the physical facilities of the unit can influence the job responsibilities of individual department chairs working on the same campus. The position of department chair is especially prone to wide variations in method for selection, delegated authority, and assigned responsibilities. On campuses where faculty are organized as a collective bargaining unit, department chairs are sometimes identified as part of, and sometimes excluded from, membership in the association.

To develop a solid understanding of the administrator's position, the mentor is likely to find it useful to check a number of sources. Read the printed position description that may appear in the faculty handbook or other campus documents. Listen to the administrator recount the issues and tasks that consume his or her time and attention. Ask questions to obtain a better grasp of the scope and level of responsibility assigned to the administrator. Often the questions the mentor asks about the position responsibilities will help the administrator organize his or her thoughts about the job. The need to explain one's responsibilities to a mentor will help the administrator acquire a third-person perspective on daily tasks.

The mentor should also examine artifacts such as accreditation reports or evaluation letters prepared by the administrator. These will help provide a sense of pressing priorities for the department whereas the administrator is likely to think first about those activities currently demanding his or her attention. For example, if the portfolio is written during that time of the year when the administrator conducts annual performance reviews of untenured faculty, this responsibility may inaccurately overshadow some of the administrator's other responsibilities.

To be effective, the mentor must be familiar with the administrator's current roles and responsibilities. The extent to which the mentor will need to gather impressions from a number of sources will depend upon the administrator's ability to objectively describe his or her responsibilities.

TASK 2. DISCUSS THE ADMINISTRATOR'S PURPOSE IN WRITING A PORTFOLIO

The purpose must be clear in the mind of the administrator, or the portfolio will be difficult to write and confusing to the reader. In some instances, the mentor may only need to learn the administrator's purpose for writing a portfolio, but in other cases the mentor will need to help the administrator decide on the primary purpose. Confusion about purpose is most likely to exist when the administrator is attempting to prepare a portfolio that will have a number of readers including, for example, a supervisor, a search committee, and an award committee. While it is possible to write a portfolio that serves more than one purpose, the administrator and the mentor need to be clear on the primary reason for preparing a portfolio. Inevitably, time will be saved in the long run if the purpose for writing a portfolio is clear before one begins to write.

TASK 3. DISCUSS THE ADMINISTRATOR'S APPROACH TO ADMINISTRATION

Typically, administrators report that writing their philosophy of administration is the toughest part of preparing a portfolio. This is not surprising since many administrators report that they rarely have an opportunity to talk about how and why they do their job as they do. The amount of time that a mentor needs to spend in discussion about the administrator's approach to the job will depend on the administrator's initial clarity in describing his or her approach to administration. If the person is reflective by nature and has amassed a significant amount of experience, he or she is likely to have a clearer sense of the philosophy than the administrator who is too new to the job or too busy with assigned tasks to reflect on style. The less clear the administrator's thoughts are about his or her approach to administration, the more important it will be to articulate such thoughts to the mentor, and the more these discussions with the mentor will make the writing easier.

The mentor should not assume a passive role in discussions about the administrator's approach. To help the administrator formulate thoughts, the mentor must engage in active listening and be ready to question the administrator's logic or views. The mentor should challenge the administrator to connect lofty thoughts or hollow assertions to concrete and specific illustrations. For example, if an administrator asserts that his or her philosophy is to be inclusive, the mentor needs to challenge the administrator to provide specific instances that illustrate this approach. The administrator needs to include in the portfolio specific references that illustrate the how and why of the administrator's approach to the job. Such specificity is important to the clarity of the portfolio and is not likely to be realized unless the mentor helps the administrator formulate his or her thoughts about the approach to administration.

These discussions help to build a constructive rapport between the administrator and the mentor. Even though the mentor was selected by the administrator to advise on writing the portfolio, it is likely that the purpose for this collaboration is new to both parties. Furthermore, the mentor's task requires his or her careful review of the administrator's writing and comments on the administrator's clarity about job performance. No matter how long the mentor and administrator have known one another, this may be a new working relationship for both individuals. The process of preparing the portfolio will move more smoothly if the mentor adopts the role of a coach rather than that of a critic. Discussion before the mentor reviews a draft will help to establish a constructive rapport between the mentor and the administrator.

TASK 4. READ THE BASIC PORTFOLIO INFORMATION

The basic information included in all administrative portfolios is the introduction, a summary of administrative responsibilities, and the administrator's approach to the job. Even when the mentor is actively involved in discussing these portfolio items, it is important to read the first draft of the basic portfolio information very carefully and from a third-person point of view. Critique the draft for clarity, coverage, and consistency. Is the document clear and easy to understand? Does it cover the position responsibilities? Is the described approach to administration consistent with performance examples? Page format, text organization, and writing style are important in that these factors contribute to the clarity of the document.

We recommend that mentors read the draft privately and not while sitting with the administrator. This will allow the mentor to move unrushed through the document. When the mentor reads in front of the administrator, the integrity of the review is sacrificed because the mentor's attention is understandably divided between the draft and the administrator. Most likely, the mentor will want to read the document two or three times before meeting with the administrator to consider suggested revisions.

The meeting to discuss the draft will work best if the mentor and administrator each have a copy of the document. The mentor should resist the temptation to trade drafts and allow the administrator to read the mentor's penned notes. Doing so will inevitably focus the administrator's attention on the stylistic suggestions, and the value of having a mentor is lost. By retaining the edited copy, the mentor can engage the administrator in an active learning process. The mentor is free to elaborate on the edited notes, and the administrator is forced to write the suggestions in his or her own words on a clean draft.

Mentors should keep the discussion focused on the substance and not on the editing notes. If the edited copy contains a lot of writing on it, the mentor will find that the conversation will be more productive if the administrator is not distracted by seeing the draft that may be covered with red ink. If the edited draft is visible, the mentor may want to begin the session with some positive comments that put the suggestions for improving the document in the larger context of working together toward a common purpose. Mentors will find it useful to keep edited drafts because they serve as an efficient aid to memory and a time saver when reviewing the next version of the portfolio.

Above all, the mentor must be honest in approaching the administrator and the draft portfolio. The mentor needs to be ready to recognize a bad situation and help the administrator face less successful activities that are referenced in the portfolio. Regardless of the purpose for writing a portfolio, the administrator is never served when areas that need improvement are ignored or glossed over. The most credible way to handle less effective behaviors and outcomes is to demonstrate that the administrator recognizes an undesirable situation and that he or she is doing something about it. The mentor needs to help the administrator understand the benefit of admitting areas targeted for improvement and presenting specific strategies to realize more success.

In some instances, the mentor will need to help alter the administrator's perspective. This is particularly important when the administrator is striving to satisfy objectives that are not the best measures of his or her job performance. For example, the mentor will need to help a chair who is focused on how much faculty like him or her to understand why being liked is not the best measure of one's effectiveness. In reviewing the portfolio draft, the mentor needs to make certain that the measures of effectiveness correspond to the administrator's position responsibilities.

TASK 5. COLLABORATE WITH THE ADMINISTRATOR ON THE ITEMS TO BE INCLUDED IN THE PORTFOLIO

The portfolio should include evidence of administrative style (behaviors) and administrative effectiveness (outcomes). Administrative style encompasses such behaviors as decision-making, planning, organizing, and communicating. The outcomes of these behaviors illustrate the administrator's effectiveness. In Chapter Five of this text, the writers offer a long list of items that the administrator may provide or secure from others that would help to document both style and effectiveness. The mentor should help the administrator decide on the particular items to be included in the portfolio with the purpose of providing a balanced picture of both style and effectiveness.

The items included in the portfolio should represent and illustrate the major responsibilities of the administrator's position. If the administrator spends 75% of his or her time on personnel matters, then roughly 75% of the items included in the portfolio would illustrate the administrator's style and effectiveness in managing personnel issues. Specific items need to be informative and easy to interpret. They should help to clarify and illustrate the responsibilities carried out by the administrator. The mentor must help the administrator resist the temptation to include an item because it is convenient and to invest the extra effort needed to gather an array of items that collectively illustrate administrative performance. The mentor keeps the administrator focused on the purpose of selecting items to be included in the portfolio to make certain that only relevant items are included.

The mentor should also help the administrator assess the merit of each item. Items might include samples of the administrator's work or qualitative and quantitative data illustrating his or her effectiveness. The administrator should resist including data for the sake of having data, and include only those data that add meaning to the narrative and the reader's understanding of the administrator's job performance. Assess the value added to the portfolio by each item considered for inclusion. Does the item contain reliable and valid data? Is the source of the data credible? Do the items included provide multiple measures of the administrator's effectiveness? It is, for example, more powerful to include the accrediting team's summary evaluation of the self-study document prepared by the chair than it would be to include the self-study document. Similarly, it is more important to include a summary of faculty evaluations of the chair's leadership than to include only the chair's goal statement for conducting department business.

Once the items are selected, the mentor should work with the administrator to organize them in appendices that correspond with the narrative of the portfolio. It is perfectly acceptable to use one item to illustrate more than one aspect of the administrator's style or effectiveness, but the portfolio narrative should clearly reference the specific item that illustrates each issue or accomplishment. The narrative explains the case, and the items in the appendices allow the reader to quickly and easily find the documentation that evidences the case being made.

Task 6. Discuss the Presentation of the Portfolio

The mentor may need to help the administrator make decisions on how best to present the portfolio. The writers recommend a three-ring binder so material can be updated or changed without redrafting the entire document. Typically the items included need to be updated every year or so, and this will be easiest to do when using a three-ring binder. By including labeled dividers, the administrator makes it easier for the reader to flip back and forth from narrative to the appendices.

The format of each page may require more thought. The mentor may need to help the administrator think about the interests of the intended reader(s). If the portfolio purpose is performance evaluation, then the narrative and appendices should be organized in a manner that allows the reader to find salient information easily. The mentor will, in most instances, need to help the administrator step back from the document and consider the appropriateness of the presentation for a reader who is unfamiliar with the material presented and possibly unfamiliar with the responsibilities of the administrator's position.

The page format should be clear and uncluttered. It should be at worst easy to read and at best inviting. The mentor will need to reinforce with the administrator the advantage of trying out several different page formats for clarity and appearance. The mentor should encourage the administrator to make full use of bold print, headings, and underlining to improve the ease of reading the portfolio and highlight the key content and salient documentation.

TASK 7. REVIEW THE DRAFT OF THE ENTIRE PORTFOLIO

After the portfolio is in final form, the mentor should read it again from a third-person perspective. This is a difficult but important read. It is difficult because the mentor is often as familiar with the content of the portfolio as is the administrator, and yet the mentor must read it as though he or she were viewing it for the first time. The mentor will find it helpful to get some distance from the portfolio by putting it aside for several days and then reading it again. It may help to read portions out loud to hear how they sound and determine if they would make sense to the new reader. Typically, any techniques that the mentor finds useful when proofreading familiar materials will help in this final task.

10

IMPLEMENTING AN ADMINISTRATIVE PORTFOLIO REVIEW PROGRAM

Colleges and universities have become accustomed to evaluating teaching, and campus policy typically prescribes that faculty collect student and peer evaluations on a regular basis. The teaching portfolio is widely used and very popular because it moves beyond the presentation of scores earned on standardized measures and builds a context for the faculty member's teaching performance. The portfolio incorporates evaluation results (outcomes) in a comprehensive but concise narrative of the faculty member's instructional philosophy, goals, and objectives. Teaching portfolios are sometimes used to support personnel decisions about tenure and promotion, but more often they are used in ongoing programs of teaching improvement.

Institutions of higher education are often less precise in their approach to administrative review. Relatively few colleges and universities maintain a program of ongoing professional development for department chairs and other academic administrators. When there is a mandatory program of administrative review, the purpose is typically to determine whether the administrator should remain in the position. University policy, for example, might stipulate that department chairs must be evaluated every three years. These performance reviews commonly solicit faculty and staff assessments of the chair's job performance on a survey instrument which is collected and read by the dean. Rarely does a campus engage in performance review of department chairs or other academic administrators for the sole purpose of improving administrative effectiveness.

The administrative portfolio can serve the same professional development purpose for administrators that the teaching portfolio provides for faculty. It also allows for a more comprehensive approach to performance evaluation. The portfolio offers a context for performance review that includes consideration of the administrator's approach and self-assessment. A supervisor is able, therefore, to review the administrator's performance in relation to that individual's administrative philosophy, goals, and strategies. The performance review afforded by the portfolio offers insights into why the administrator performs as he or she does. This information enables the evaluator to know better how to assist the administrator by pointing out the specific behavioral changes that are needed to improve performance and effectiveness.

The portfolio helps the administrator focus on improving job performance in between the formal reviews prescribed by campus policy. It has the advantage of helping the administrator develop the practice of continuously revisiting performance and reflecting on what might be done differently to enhance one's effectiveness. Administrators who have prepared a portfolio report that the exercise of compiling and updating one's portfolio provides a structure and process for continuously thinking about how to improve their administrative effectiveness.

A program of administrative portfolio review serves the administrator and the institution because it responds to the need for performance evaluation, facilitates performance improvement, and sustains professional development. In this chapter, the writers describe a process by which an institution can implement a program of administrative portfolio review and delineate the advantages of doing so.

BUILD CONSENSUS FOR INVESTING TIME ON ADMINISTRATIVE DEVELOPMENT

Often department chairs, program directors, and other frontline academic administrators view their administrative role as separate from their real work. Administrators who view their role as temporary or somehow separate from their real work are less likely to invest time developing their skills. Some administrators may be too focused on getting the job done to think about professional development or to engage in the reflection necessary to enhance their effectiveness. But institutions of higher education need academic administrators at all levels of the institution to be as effective as possible in performing their assigned duties, including department chairs serving a temporary three-year term.

Hiring officials can establish the expectation for continuous improvement at all levels of the institution during the interview of a candidate. Most applicants will appreciate a supervisor who wants them to succeed, and it is easier to discuss performance evaluation as a component of professional development during the search process than it is after a person is hired and especially after the administrator has encountered some difficulties in carrying out assigned responsibilities.

Similarly, the portfolio method will be more easily implemented on campus if it is not initiated in response to some specific problematic occurrence, but as a vehicle for helping administrators be more successful. Few administrators will resist the institution's investment in their success if they understand the personal benefits of writing a portfolio. Resistance is most likely to occur when the administrator perceives the portfolio as a purely summative evaluative technique. Consequently, an important step in implementing a program of administrative portfolio review is to build consensus around the intrinsic benefits of ongoing professional development for administrators.

Some administrators will reflexively resist portfolio development if they do not see the exercise of writing a portfolio as contributing to their overall success. As explained in Chapter Seven, the administrative portfolio is not about developing defensive documentation that becomes useful should the administrator's decisions or approach be challenged. Rather, the portfolio is about honest reflection that leads to informed leadership. Preparing a portfolio allows the administrator to step back from the immediate pressures of the job to obtain the enlightened view that can only come from a third-person perspective. Done correctly, preparing a portfolio is never busywork.

Presenting the portfolio as a vehicle for documenting positive contributions should appeal to administrators who are experiencing the increased pressure for administrative accountability. The portfolio enables the administrator to explain how and why he or she carries out assigned responsibilities. Because the portfolio is reviewed by the administrator's supervisor, the administrator can continue with the comfort of knowing that the supervisor understands and endorses the administrator's approach. If the supervisor disagrees with any goal or strategy described in the portfolio, he or she can discuss it with the administrator in advance of a specific incident. Hence the portfolio keeps the administrator and his or her supervisor on the same page.

To build consensus for investing in professional development for administrators, the institutional leadership must acknowledge individual as well as institutional benefits from continuous professional development for administrators. The unique benefit of the portfolio is that it structures a contextual approach to performance evaluation and focuses attention on improving administrative performance. The portfolio offers a constructive process that engages the administrator in a reflective process that can serve both summative and formative purposes for the individual administrator and the campus.

CLARIFY ROLE RESPONSIBILITIES AND PERFORMANCE EXPECTATIONS

It is virtually impossible to evaluate the administrator's effectiveness if performance expectations are not clear (Higgerson, 1996). Often the supervisor's dissatisfaction with performance and the administrator's reported frustration with a job are attributable to unclear position responsibilities. Supervisors cannot assume that a detailed position description is sufficient to an individual's complete understanding of role responsibilities and performance expectations. The position description for a department chair, for example, is likely to state that the chair is responsible for faculty development. This one responsibility can connote an array of performance expectations. For example, does the responsibility start and stop with the expectation that the chair will conduct annual performance evaluations sessions with each faculty member? Or does the responsibility carry more performance expectations that include ongoing mentoring activities?

Job satisfaction and performance improvement build from a clear understanding of one's roles and responsibilities as well as performance expectations. The administrative portfolio provides the opportunity for a structured conversation about these important issues. More importantly, because the portfolio offers a contextual understanding of what the administrator does and why, it allows for a nondefensive discussion that enhances the likelihood of improvement.

INTRODUCE THE PORTFOLIO AS A VEHICLE FOR REALIZING INDIVIDUAL PROFESSIONAL DEVELOPMENT

The advantage of the portfolio is that it moves beyond performance evaluation to allow for a contextual and comprehensive approach to professional development. It would be inaccurate and misleading to introduce the administrative portfolio with a focus on only the evaluation of performance. Instead, the portfolio should be introduced as a program that satisfies both individual and campus needs for performance evaluation and ongoing professional development.

Administrators need to understand that writing a personal portfolio allows for contextual performance evaluation. Done correctly, the portfolio should reduce the dread sometimes associated with performance evaluation for the administrator and his or her supervisor because with the portfolio administrative decisions and outcomes are explained in the context of why the administrator acted as he or she did. Consequently, the portfolio provides a structure for reflection which is essential to purposeful professional development.

Administrative jobs are increasingly complex, and often individuals have little or no prior training on how to manage all of their assigned tasks. In some instances, a person is hired into an academic administrative position on the basis of criteria that are very different from the skills needed to do the job. Department chairs, for example, may be selected on the basis of their research and publication, when the skills needed to chair an academic department today require a knowledge and skill base that is different from the qualifications that lend themselves to becoming a published scholar.

The portfolio facilitates individual professional development by identifying areas of strengths and needed improvement. Because the important realizations are made in relation to the administrator's assigned responsibilities, the portfolio is a very efficient tool for enhancing administrative success.

Illustrate the Value of Professional Development to the Health of the Institution

Professional development is essential to the health of the institution because a campus is a living organization that must evolve and grow. This requires honest reflection about what the leadership is doing and why. It requires a willingness to consider new and different ways of carrying out assigned responsibilities. If institutions are to stay the course of continuous improvement, administrators at all levels need clear performance goals that advance the institution's mission. They also need the focus and support provided by a continuous focus on professional development.

An institution benefits from improving individual administrators' proficiency for self-assessment. Individual administrators need to develop a facility for taking a third-person perspective on their job performance. This requires them to step back from the first-person participant perspective to evaluate what they are doing and why from the vantage point of a third-person observer. Administrators who are resistant to performance evaluation can usually recognize the advantage of taking time out to engage in their own third-person perspective assessment of what they do and why and whether their efforts yield the desired results. An administrative portfolio review program establishes a structure that makes this happen.

ADDRESS SPECIFIC CONCERNS

Implementing a portfolio review program represents change, and change can be uncomfortable for many. Higgerson (1996, p. 177) explains that "any person's first reaction to proposed change will be to ask how it affects him or her in terms of job security, opportunity for professional advancement, promotion, salary increase, workload, and the like." Frequent communication with administrators before, during, and after the implementation of the portfolio review program can help alleviate personal concerns. Higgerson warns that "during any change effort, rumors tend to run rampant." The extent to which individuals believe that their specific concerns are heard and addressed will reduce their resistance to change and minimize unfounded fears that jeopardize the successful implementation of a portfolio review program.

If, for example, chairs express a concern that writing a portfolio will take too much time, it will be ineffective to discuss only the advantages of writing a portfolio. It will be essential to address the time needed to write the portfolio. The time concern may be addressed by describing the time commitment that is discussed in Chapter Five of this text and by noting the available support that will make the task easier. Support might include, for example, models of other portfolios or the availability of trained portfolio mentors. Effective implementation of a portfolio review program requires that those charged with implementing the initiative hear and respond to the specific issues and concerns raised by the administrators.

The process of addressing individual concerns regarding the implementation of a new initiative can be helped by presenting expert testimony. In this instance, administrators will find it useful to hear from others who have written portfolios. These may be individuals from other institutions or a few who took part in a pilot program at the home campus. In this text, one such source is offered in Chapter Twelve in a contribution by Deborah DeZure. Also, in Chapter Six, the writers offer quotes from administrators who have written portfolios.

If administrators remain resistant to the implementation of a portfolio review program, the writers recommend seeking their support to try it on an experimental basis. Establish the time frame for the experimental trial, and agree on the criteria to be used in evaluating the effectiveness of the portfolio review program. The criteria should encompass the specific concerns held by the more resistant administrators as well as the anticipated benefits of the program. It is especially important that the timetable for the experimental trial be honored and that the review take place on the agreed upon date. This approach allows resistant individuals to experience the benefits of writing a portfolio while knowing that, if the investment proves not to be worth the benefits, the program need not become permanent.

FACILITATE THE PORTFOLIO WRITING PROCESS BY PROVIDING MODELS AND MENTORS

If the concerns are of a practical, logistical nature, it may be necessary to be very concrete about the support available for writing a portfolio. It is important to provide administrators with sample portfolios. The samples should not be all from individuals who occupy the same or similar position, but should include portfolios written by administrators who occupy positions higher and lower in the institution. Using models from within the institution can have the added benefit of bridging misunderstandings about different roles and corresponding responsibilities. Sometimes it is helpful for more senior administrators to model professional development by leading in the writing of administrative portfolios. In this text, the writers provide numerous sample portfolios that span a number of position titles, disciplines, and institution types.

It may be desirable to seek external support for coaching the portfolio writing. Such support can come in the form of portfolio mentors who may work in other units on the same campus or who may work at different institutions. Each model of providing mentor support carries advantages and costs that need to be assessed in relation to the specific needs of the institution. For example, if the campus culture is healthy and generally supportive of the need to engage in ongoing professional development, then administrators can probably serve as portfolio coaches for one another. If, however, the campus climate is more resistant to professional development and there exists a significant degree of skepticism or paranoia about the purpose for implementing a portfolio review program, then it is preferable to seek portfolios mentors from outside the campus. When using untrained portfolio mentors, it will be especially important to use the material provided in Chapter Nine of this text to coach them on how to be a portfolio mentor.

REFERENCE

Higgerson, M. L. (1996). *Communication skills for department chairs.* Bolton, MA: Anker.

11

SPECIAL QUESTIONS, CONCERNS, AND ISSUES

The purpose for writing an administrative portfolio varies with individual administrators. The portfolio allows the administrator to organize and present content that is unique to his or her purpose and professional situation. The portfolio does not prescribe a standard format or outline to which all administrators must mold their presentation. In this chapter, the writers address some of the nontraditional purposes and approaches to writing a portfolio. A question-and-answer format is used to aid the administrator in finding those issues and concerns that have personal relevance without needing to read the entire chapter.

IS THERE ANY VALUE IN WRITING A PORTFOLIO IF THE ADMINISTRATOR IS THE ONLY PERSON WHO IS LIKELY TO READ IT?

Many administrators who write portfolios tell us that a primary value in writing a portfolio is the personal benefit derived from engaging in portfolio development. The portfolio provides an opportunity for structured and systematic reflection about one's assigned responsibilities and job performance. The administrator is forced to think about administrative duties and strategies. There is no better vehicle for making a comprehensive assessment of the administrator's professional status and effectiveness. Such introspection is essential to identifying the cognitive and skill components that need further development.

The contextual presentation of the administrator's role, responsibilities, and effectiveness that is provided through the portfolio can help the administrator recognize and escape being stuck in a career pothole. The portfolio coaches the administrator through the important questions that must be answered in order to decide how best to evolve one's career. The portfolio guides continued professional development by building a context for understanding one's current administrative responsibilities and abilities.

It is likely that the administrator will want to have others read the portfolio once it is written. The portfolio can serve as a conversation starter for the administrator who would otherwise find it difficult to engage others in a discussion about his or her professional development and career aspirations. The portfolio format enables the administrator to secure the important reaction of others without a lengthy oral presentation of position duties or the administrator's approach to them because the information is contained in the portfolio. This feedback is helpful to navigating career decisions.

IS THERE ANY VALUE IN WRITING A PORTFOLIO WHEN THE ADMINISTRATOR IS PLACEBOUND AND THERE IS NO CAMPUS REQUIREMENT FOR ADMINISTRATIVE REVIEW?

Often individuals who are placebound find that they are stereotyped on their campus as being best suited for a particular type of administrative position. An administrator, for example, may discover that he or she has a difficult time moving from staff positions such as assistant chair or associate dean to positions with line authority such as department chair or division head. Because the portfolio displays the administrator's philosophy and strategies, writing it can be useful in dispelling stereotypes by helping others perceive the administrator as ready to assume more or different administrative responsibilities. In this case, the administrator would want to invite significant individuals to read the portfolio even though there may not be a campus policy that requires the evaluation of administrative performance. Because the portfolio brings together in one place information about the scope and quality of the administrator's activities, it enables the administrator to discuss his or her readiness for assuming greater responsibilities from a position of strength because the conversation is informed by the portfolio account of the administrator's job performance. This approach is eminently more effective than merely asking for different duties or a more challenging administrative position.

Is There Any Value in Writing a Portfolio When the Administrator Is Not Sure of His or Her Career Aspirations?

The portfolio can help the administrator discover groupings of preferred and dreaded job responsibilities. It also allows the administrator to assess his or her strengths and weaknesses as they relate to administrative tasks. By doing so, the portfolio can help the administrator discover such important information as his or her best fit. Because the portfolio builds a context for understanding the administrator's job performance, it typically offers insights on one's best fit for the type of position and institution. For example, the administrator may discover that he or she is better in working with the full-time faculty than with a large contingent of part-time faculty. This information can be useful in determining the type of institution where the administrator would prefer to work.

Writing a portfolio can help the administrator discover specific information about his or her job performance and preferences that is essential to making career decisions. It can offer guidance on both the type of position and institution that would best fit the administrator's experience and skill. This clarity is important to conducting a successful search for a new position. Furthermore, the portfolio will typically contain information that is likely to be requested by the search committee, so writing the portfolio moves the uncertain administrator one step closer to finding the perfect next position.

Is There Any Value in Writing a Portfolio if the Administrator Does Not Plan to Change Jobs?

As explained in Chapter One, today's academic administrator must manage complex duties, and this requires a diverse skill base. Writing a portfolio can help an administrator identify those areas that need more professional development. Improving one's skill base will inevitably increase the administrator's comfort in performing assigned responsibilities. A portfolio differs dramatically from the annual department report in that it includes the how and why of administrative performance. It is the why you do what you do that offers insight on the administrator's specific skill needs. A department chair, for example, might discover that he or she spends significantly more time working with untenured faculty than with tenured faculty on professional development even though the chair has responsibility for attending to the professional development of all department faculty. Performance improvement becomes possible when the administrator is confronted with portfolio data that illustrate strengths and weaknesses. Portfolio data are more compelling than other sources because they derive from sources that the administrator accepts as being fair and accurate.

WILL IMPLEMENTING AN ADMINISTRATIVE PORTFOLIO PROGRAM READY ADMINISTRATORS TO LEAVE THE INSTITUTION?

Perhaps, but it is also likely that implementing an administrative portfolio program will enable the institution to retain effective administrators. Because the portfolio centers on professional development, it demonstrates the institution's investment in the continued professional improvement of individual administrators. A portfolio program provides administrators with a self-directed vehicle for continued growth and nurturing. It facilitates ongoing discussions about performance improvement that are likely to increase the administrator's job comfort and satisfaction.

The administrative portfolio offers a win-win approach to performance evaluation. The institution gains a comprehensive program of performance review that will more likely result in enhanced performance. The administrator benefits from insights and professional development support not typically realized in other programs of performance review.

REFLECTIONS ON DEVELOPING AN ADMINISTRATIVE PORTFOLIO

Deborah DeZure

CLARIFYING PURPOSES

In 1996, when Peter Seldin and I first discussed collaborating on the development of an administrative portfolio, we had different but complementary goals. Peter wanted to develop a new prototype that would adapt the teaching portfolio model to the evaluation of administrators in higher education. He believed that the portfolio and the process by which it was developed offered a useful vehicle for administrators both to document and to improve their practice.

I had professional and personal reasons to develop an administrative portfolio. Serving as director of a teaching center at a large university, I was a senior administrator with annual requirements to evaluate, document, and report my work to the provost and vice president for academic affairs and to the teaching center's advisory board. The prescribed approach to evaluating senior administrators was based on more traditional academic roles, including department heads, deans, and vice presidents. I welcomed an opportunity to design an approach to assessment that I could tailor to what I actually did and to the extended time frame within which those efforts were likely to reach fruition.

I also felt it was important to develop a portfolio of my own work because, like many faculty developers, I was actively promoting the use of teaching portfolios. I wanted to model what I advocated for faculty, even if it meant adapting the teaching portfolio to my work as an administrator. And finally, I knew that, at some point, I would want to explore positions outside that institution. I anticipated the need to clarify the nature of my responsibilities to search committees that might be unfamiliar with the work of faculty and instructional developers.

Fueled by the assessment movement in the mid-1990s, higher education itself was focused on new multidimensional approaches to evaluation. The fundamental conception of evaluation was changing, with increased emphasis on self-assessment and reflection to promote growth and development, not simply on evaluation of past performance. New approaches also emphasized evaluation as an active partnership in which you had input, choice, and agency, empowering individuals to include items and issues that they valued and that reflected the richness and diversity of their professional lives.

For all these reasons, the time seemed right to adapt the teaching portfolio to the work of administrators.

DEVELOPING THE ADMINISTRATIVE PORTFOLIO

Defining Process

In 1997, Peter Seldin and I embarked on the process of developing a prototype of an administrative portfolio. Peter would serve as my mentor, drawing on his extensive experience with teaching portfolios. I would provide the content for the prototype, drawing on my work as director of a teaching center for the past six years. Together, we would then reflect on both the process and the product and assess their utility for other administrators in higher education. There was an experimental quality to this venture, adding both the exhilaration of traversing new ground and the risks that go along with any voyage into the unknown.

The process of preparing a portfolio was a quest to clarify both to myself and to others what I do, how, why, and what impact I had in my administrative role. But even beyond those factors, I hoped it would provide an opportunity to explore my beliefs about leadership: the theories and principles that lay behind my decisions and practices. For years I had promoted the concept of praxis—the convergence of theory and practice in what faculty do—whether it was in their roles as instructors, researchers, or practitioners across the disciplines. Here was my opportunity to document the ways in which my own practice as an administrator was informed by the theories, principles, and values I had long embraced or evolved through experience. While I had often thought about these issues, I had never systematically tried to trace their connection, nor had I ever attempted to write them down and codify them as a consistent approach to what I do. I also wondered about the disjuncture and inconsistencies that might exist between what I believe and what I do. And if there were inconsistencies, were they a result of compromises made to deal with limited resources (that is, were they the best I could do within the constraints), or were they active choices that were incompatible with my beliefs and in need of review and revision? For me, the issue of praxis appeared to be both the greatest challenge and the one I was most eager to confront.

Knowing the Audience

The beginning steps were straightforward. The first of these was to clarify the audiences for whom the portfolio was intended. I had two primary audiences: the provost and vice president for academic affairs to whom I had a direct reporting relationship and the teaching center's advisory board, consisting of 30 faculty and administrators from across the disciplines and divisions of the university. I also had two secondary and less immediate audiences: possible future employers (although at the time I had no thoughts of changing positions) and other faculty developers who might appreciate a new model to use for evaluation of their work.

Determining Which Sections to Include

Peter and I then turned to the task of identifying a tentative list of sections that my portfolio should include. The list was a crossbreed of a teaching portfolio, an administrator's performance review, and an annual report for a service unit. The table of contents is included in Figure 12.1.

The section that generated the most discussion between my mentor and myself was the section on the Five Most Significant Accomplishments During the Director's Term. This had no analogue in the teaching portfolio, but it was characteristic of the norms of reporting on my campus. Indeed, every annual performance review I had had as director focused specifically on the question of what were the most significant accomplishments since the past review. If I was tailoring this document to the audiences who would read it, I needed to include sections that my reviewers would value and want to see. In the end, we agreed that it was both appropriate and useful to include this section in my portfolio. I mention our deliberations about whether to include this section to underscore the need to customize the list of suggested sections or topics to reflect your needs, local norms, and audience expectations.

Collecting and Preparing the Evidence

As I reviewed the list of sections, I realized that I had already collected documentation and evidence for most sections in anticipation of my yearly personal performance review and my unit's annual report. Some of the materials

Figure 12.1

FACULTY DEVELOPER PORTFOLIO

Deborah DeZure
Director, Faculty Center for Instructional Excellence (FCIE)
Eastern Michigan University, Ypsilanti, MI
October 1997

Table of Contents

Introduction: Purpose, Institutional Context, The Faculty Center for Instructional Excellence (FCIE)
Instructional Development Responsibilities
Philosophy: Guiding Principles
Assessing Faculty Instructional Needs
Workshops/Services/Programs Organized and/or Presented by the Developer
Research and Publications: For Internal and External Use
Grants: Awarded to the FCIE and offered by the FCIE
Participation on University Committees
Evidence of Impact on Teaching and Learning
Areas for Improvement
Five Most Significant Accomplishments During the Director's Term

Appendices

- *FCIE Fall 1997 Services and Events Calendar*
- FCIE Newsletter: *Whys and Ways of Teaching*
- Video and Manual—*Sharing Learning Expectations: What Students Want from College Teachers*
- *FCIE Annual Report 1996–1997*
- FCIE Evaluation Form
- FCIE Advisory Board Evaluation Form

would need to be reconfigured for the administrator portfolio, but they were readily available and took only a few hours to retrieve. Organizing and editing the materials would take longer.

The sections that were new for me and would require considerable reflection as well as time to write would be the sections on the Philosophy of Practice and Areas for Improvement. I had certainly deliberated about these issues a great deal, but I had never organized my thoughts on them, nor had I committed them to paper for me or others to read.

It was a source of both humor and consternation when I realized that the only time I had ever been asked about my philosophy of practice was during my initial job interview. I had opportunities to clarify some of my principles of practice when I oriented new members of the teaching center's advisory board each year, but the statements were cursory and disembodied from a coherent view of my philosophy of practice as an administrator. The administrative portfolio offered the opportunity to articulate what I believed and to examine just how coherent and useful it had been in guiding my practices and effectiveness.

In drafting my statement of philosophy, I quickly realized that there were subtopics that would have to be addressed and that no single coherent view would clarify my principles. Instead, I started by listing my Guiding Principles of Practice. The field of faculty development itself draws upon theory, research, and best practices from several disciplines, and many of them were represented. My initial list had almost 40 guiding principles. I clustered them into three broader areas: Principles of Change in Higher Education, View of the Instructional Developer's Role, and Principles of Instructional Development Practice. They would be the basis for my statement of philosophy.

Little did I know at the time that the list of guiding principles I developed for my portfolio would be so useful to other faculty developers. They were eager to see principles of practice articulated in this way, to discuss and scrutinize them, to share them with novitiates in the field, and to test their efficacy through research. At the time that I wrote them, I was simply trying to document the principles that informed my practice. I knew that they drew upon the theory, research, and best practices in the field and on my own experience as a developer. But I could not have anticipated how useful they would be to others in my field until I began to share them at conferences, workshops for new faculty developers, and in publications.

The section on Areas for Improvement represented a different kind of challenge. I had a sense of my strengths and my weaknesses as a faculty developer because I engaged in self-reflection and self-assessment, but sharing areas for improvement with my supervisor and my colleagues was another matter. I had to think long and hard about this and concluded that the portfolio format gave me ample opportunity to reveal my strengths so that my weaknesses could be seen in a larger context of accomplishments. On balance, the risks seemed relatively low, and the benefits were quite worthwhile.

One further section deserves commentary here: the section on Evidence of Impact on Teaching and Learning—which is particularly important but problematic. Finding ways to document the impact of faculty development services on teaching and learning is extremely difficult. Many faculty development centers, including the FCIE, have a long history of documenting levels of participation and faculty satisfaction with programs and services, but documenting impact on teaching and learning outcomes is far more complex. These efforts are complicated by 1) numerous intervening variables beyond faculty development that could account for improved teaching and learning, 2) traditions of guaranteed confidentiality in faculty development services, and 3) patterns of voluntary participation in faculty development programs that inhibit requests for information about the impact of those services. The field of faculty development continues to grapple with effective ways to document impact. Progress has been made, but serious efforts were just beginning in 1997 when I developed my first administrative portfolio. Ultimately, I documented what I could and provided an introduction that explained the difficulties in providing evidence of impact.

The Length of a Portfolio

This may seem like a clear-cut issue, but it was not. When I reviewed the list of sections to include and considered the extensive evidence I had to support each one, I envisioned a document of 20 pages of narrative followed by appendices. Peter, as an experienced mentor, knew that most reviewers would want to read no more than ten pages of narrative followed by appendices. We compromised on 12 pages of narrative, but the process of winnowing it down to that length was an ongoing challenge, one in which the role of the mentor was indispensable. My first draft was much longer than either of us wanted, but it offered a place to begin the discussion of what was most valuable to include. Feedback from the mentor on successive drafts enabled me to cut judiciously and to select a representative array of evidence and discussion that was neither redundant nor disjointed.

Having an objective consultant was useful in helping me to think through and edit a document that was so personally meaningful to me and leaden with the risks inherent in evaluation. As an effective mentor, Peter raised salient and probing questions, leaving the answers and the editing to me. But the product was clearly the result of a collaboration, and it was all the stronger for it.

OBSERVATIONS ON DEVELOPING A PORTFOLIO

How Different Is a Portfolio?

Like many administrators, every year I was asked to write an annual report documenting the activities and impact of my unit. Is a portfolio really that different? Yes, it is different in several fundamental ways. First, an administrative portfolio documents the work of an individual; second, it is highly personal; third, it provides a venue to reveal your philosophy of practice and how you transform your principles and theories into practice; and last but not least, the process for developing a portfolio—when based on the involvement of a mentor—augments the opportunities for growth and reflection while enhancing the final product.

The biggest distinction between a portfolio and either a performance review or an annual report is that a portfolio is the highly personal document of an individual. It reveals beliefs and values, relationships, effort, and intent. All too often, performance reviews focus heavily if not exclusively on outcomes—that is, on product rather than process. The portfolio model makes space, literally and figuratively, for personal revelation and reflection, areas of achievement, and areas in need of further growth and development. A performance review or annual report may tell you what was accomplished, but a portfolio will tell you how it was done, by whom, to what end, and why it was a major accomplishment. These are qualitatively different approaches to evaluation. Performance reviews, annual reports, and portfolios each serve important purposes, but the portfolio addresses dimensions that are not generally included in other forms of evaluation.

A year or so ago, administrators at another institution invited me to apply for a position at their teaching center. I was asked to submit both my administrative portfolio and my traditional vita. During the interview process, I was asked several questions on the basis of my portfolio. I later asked why the portfolio was used rather than the vita as the basis for their questions. I was told that the vita conveyed what was essentially public knowledge, the information that most of them already knew about me even before they had asked me to apply: my educational background, publications, presentations, and employment history. It was the kind of information that was sufficient to warrant an invitation to apply. But the portfolio offered the personal information that they would use to assess if I was the kind of professional and person they wanted as a colleague. It revealed my professional values and the way I think about my discipline (in this case, faculty development). It spoke in my own voice of my strengths, my areas in need of improvement, and why I valued and selected each of the Five Major Accomplishments. None of that was evident from my vita.

I was offered the position and am now Coordinator of Faculty Programs at the Center for Learning and Teaching at the University of Michigan, Ann Arbor. When I developed my portfolio, I had no idea it would indeed facilitate my ability to find a new position. At the time, finding a new position had been only a remote goal, but even then I realized that developing a portfolio is a commitment to one's own growth. It is also a commitment that makes so much else possible.

When Peter and I embarked on this process, we had a few simple goals: to see whether the teaching portfolio could be adapted successfully for administrators, to design a new model that was nonprescriptive and flexible enough to accommodate a variety of roles and purposes, and to utilize the model of an active partnership between administrator and mentor throughout the development process. What we found was that the model of the teaching portfolio was easy to adapt to administrator needs because of its flexibility. The process of having a mentor facilitated both the adaptation of the model and the successful completion of the administrative portfolio just as it has done in the past.

Unlike the teaching portfolio that is used to document teaching effectiveness and augment the ubiquitous reliance on student evaluations, the administrative portfolio emerges against a backdrop of longstanding traditions and paradigms of annual reports and performance reviews. If administrators are going to be asked to embrace this new form of assessment, it will have to offer something unique and worthy of their time and effort: The value-added will have to be very significant. I think it is. The portfolio captures aspects of one's professional life that are not addressed by other forms of administrator evaluation. The form changes the function, and in doing so it may even change the conceptions, discourse, and expectations about evaluation. The portfolio offers opportunities for those who want new ways to view their life's work, and it offers the field of higher education a viable and productive alternative to augment other evaluation models.

I'll conclude this essay with a brief story. When I was a child, my uncle Charley used to ask each of his nieces and nephews, "And what is it you stand for?" As children, none of us knew what he meant or how to respond. We'd laugh nervously, sensing that the question was important, but that the answer lay well beyond our reach. Nonetheless, even then we knew he was planting a seed for the future. Over the years, from time to time, I would ponder Charley's question knowing that the answer was still inchoate, just beneath the surface. And yet, when I completed my portfolio, I remember thinking, "Uncle Charley, *this* is what I stand for." Both the process of creating a portfolio and the product had enabled me to address that important question.

A portfolio is not a panacea. You'll get out of it in direct proportion to what you put into it. But for those who are willing to engage in a quest of self-discovery, a portfolio does offer a compelling vehicle to explore and reveal our professional lives and who we have become. In the context of academic life, that is saying a lot.

PART II

Sample Administrative Portfolios

Part II is comprised of 13 sample portfolios from across administrative positions. They have been prepared by administrators at Baldwin-Wallace College (Ohio); Columbia College (South Carolina); Columbus State University (Georgia); Harrisburg Area Community College (Pennsylvania); James Madison University (Virginia); Rutgers University (New Jersey); the University of Akron (Ohio); the University of Missouri, Kansas City; the University of Northern Iowa; and the University of Wisconsin, Stevens Point.

The appendix material referred to, though part of the actual portfolios, is not included because of its cumbersome nature.

Because each portfolio is an individualized document, varying importance has been assigned by different administrators to different items. Some administrators discuss an item at length; others dismiss it with just a sentence or two, or even omit it. IMPORTANT NOTE: Readers are urged to remember that institutions differ in their use of administrative titles. Administrators with similar duties and responsibilities may well have different titles.

Virtually all of the administrators whose portfolios appear here, regardless of title, are engaged in some common tasks. Among others, they include planning, leadership, communication, motivation, decision-making, budget, performance appraisal, and faculty or professional development.

For that reason, readers are urged to bear in mind that reading sample portfolios not of your administrative title often provides especially helpful information and insights applicable to your own position.

THE PORTFOLIOS (ARRANGED ALPHABETICALLY BY INSTITUTION)

Baldwin-Wallace College
Lee Bash, Dean, Division of Lifelong Learning
Catherine Jarjisian, Director, Conservatory of Music
G. Andrew Mickley, Chair, Department of Psychology

Columbia College
John Zubizarreta, Dean of Undergraduate Studies, Director of Honors and Faculty Development

Columbus State University
Joyce Hickson, Chair, Department of Counseling and Educational Leadership

Harrisburg Area Community College
Cathryn Amdahl, Writing Program Coordinator

James Madison University
Jane S. Halonen, Director, School of Psychology

Rutgers University
Monica A. Devanas, Director of Faculty Development and Assessment Programs

The University of Akron
Christina DePaul, Director, Myers School of Art
William K. Guegold, Director, School of Music

University of Missouri, Kansas City
Laurence D. Kaptain, Assistant Provost, Academic Affairs

University of Northern Iowa
G. Roger Sell, Director, Center for the Enhancement of Teaching

University of Wisconsin, Stevens Point
Joan DeGuire North, Dean, College of Professional Studies

ADMINISTRATIVE PORTFOLIO
Lee Bash
Dean, Division of Lifelong Learning
Baldwin-Wallace College
March 2001

Table of Contents

Introduction

Purpose. The purpose of this portfolio is to provide evidence of my efforts to be a transformative leader, reflected in my role as Dean of the Division of Lifelong Learning (LL) at Baldwin-Wallace College (B-W). While I seek formative evaluation as a result of this portfolio—the sort of feedback that will assist me to improve and grow—I also expect to benefit from the pursuit of self-reflection and self-assessment, especially through ongoing, semi-annual updates and comparisons.

Institutional context. B-W is a private liberal arts school with a total enrollment of approximately 4,800 students. At this time, the college has redefined its mission and is in the midst of implementing a new major strategic planning initiative. The adult learner has been identified as a critical component in the school's future, and lifelong learning has been embraced as an objective for all learners through its inclusion in the mission statement. B-W's adult degree-completion enrollment is currently about 850 students, down from a peak of more than 1,400 students in 1992.

Division of Lifelong Learning. As one program in Academic Affairs, LL actively seeks to employ learning opportunities for students from birth to post-retirement. Adult degree completion is central to LL's mission, as administered by its primary unit, the Evening and Weekend College. Additional LL units include the Institute for Learning in Retirement (ILR), a non-credit program for senior citizens; Professional Development, a non-credit program primarily emphasizing seminar and workshop presentations in business; and Outreach Partnerships, where LL assists and supports various campus programs and initiatives, typically intended for, but not restricted to, pre-college-aged students (the conservatory's kindermusik and preparatory programs are examples). In addition, LL administers B-W's satellite campus, Baldwin-Wallace East (BWE) where it currently offers a number of certificates and is about to introduce a degree completion program to serve what it believes is a significant potential student population.

Administrative Responsibilities
The components of my position are complex and highly interactive. I tend to view my approach from a holistic perspective that utilizes the diverse responsibilities reflected in the simple time distribution indicated in Table 1 below. Specifically, as Dean of the Division of Lifelong Learning, I:

Provide leadership and vision concerning the overall LL program for all of its constituents to help them understand where we are going and how we fit into the B-W mission. The 20 months I have been at B-W can best be characterized as change-laden. As a result, LL established weekly senior staff meetings and monthly staff meetings—to achieve information sharing and a sense of ownership among all stakeholders. Outside the division, I strive to achieve this through speeches, meetings, correspondence, and presentations—both on- and off-campus (see Appendix A). Topics comprise variations of the emerging role of adult learners in the 21st century and/or how B-W will provide leadership to respond to the needs of this population. Audiences extend from the LL staff to area fraternal groups or the community-at-large via media coverage.

Table 1

Percentage of Time Devoted to Various Responsibilities

Responsibility	%
Provide Leadership & Vision	22%
Assign & Support Staff	43%
Develop Non-credit Programs	7%
Advise ASL	3%
Manage & Oversee Staff	13%
Natl. Conferences & Journals	4%
Serve on Committees	8%

Support each staff member by assigning special and ongoing projects that will promote his or her growth and development while reflecting that person's interests because I view my success as dependent upon the skills and knowledge of my staff. Furthermore, I meet with groups of senior staff weekly and office staff monthly to maintain open communication and promote a sense of ownership. In most instances, a project is an individual's responsibility, but all projects are highly interactive—with constant feedback and exchanges of ideas. Typical ongoing projects include:

- **Schedule maintenance** for everything from faculty assignments to location and time(s), this task demands ongoing attention to a wide array of details that are distributed among the entire staff

- **Internal publications,** including adult-exclusive schedules for each term, handbooks for both faculty and students, promotional pieces that convey the image and mission of the division, special pieces for external projects, and documents designed to support new initiatives (see Appendix B)

- **New curricular initiatives** that reflect my commitment to quality and the best practices for adult learners—including new courses, schedule formats, forms of course delivery, and policies (see Appendix C)

- **New majors, certificates, programs, and outreach efforts** to broaden our enrollment at the for-credit and not-for-credit levels (see Appendix D)

- **Constant feedback** gained through the ongoing use of focus groups, both internally-designed and nationally-normed surveys, and exit interviews to determine how to improve and market our programs in a rapidly changing environment (see Appendix E)

Assist non-credit programs

- Assist and sustain the non-credit programs that form a portion of Lifelong Learning (e.g., ILR, outreach, and professional development) in order to maximize their vitality and enrollments (see Appendix F)

Serve as advisor for Alpha Sigma Lambda, the national honor society for adult learners;

Manage and oversee a staff of more than 20 individuals and an annual budget exceeding one million dollars

Attend, write for, and present at national conferences, especially those focusing on leadership and the adult learner (see Appendix G)

Serve on campus, community, and national committees to further the institution's mission in any capacity required (see Appendix H)

Professional Development Initiatives
Although my pursuit of becoming a transformative leader did not begin when I arrived at B-W, the institution has supported and encouraged my further development in this direction. During my 20 months at B-W, I have attended 11 national and international conferences, at five of which I presented papers. Furthermore, I was selected to serve as a consultant-evaluator by the North Central Association Higher Learning Commission—an opportunity I value since it enables me to take part in the peer review process at the highest level. At the same time, it allows me to gain a broader critical perspective and understanding of various institutions of higher education.

In addition, I was selected to participate in Harvard University's Institute for Higher Education MLE program. This intensive two-week institute gave me exposure to a host of prominent leadership experts and provided me with a rich network of associates from among my classmates whom I can call upon for advice and assistance.

Finally, I was honored by the Association of American Colleges and Universities (AAC&U) recently when a B-W team I proposed leading was selected to participate in their Campus Leadership for Sustainable Innovation one-week institute. This is a part of AAC&U's Greater Expectations Initiative that examines the aims and practices of a 21st century undergraduate education. It is intended to assemble teams from many of the leading colleges in America to discuss this topic, and therefore, I anticipate expanding the dialogue on the B-W campus when it comes to curricular reform and best practices.

Statement of Administrative Philosophy

My administrative philosophy is reflected by the two challenges I face in my position as Dean of LL: The first (more global)—turning vision into action through leadership—remains a constant companion in my long search for mastery as a transformative leader; the second (more topical)—maintaining balance between the competing needs expressed by adult students and the concerns presented by the faculty—affirms my pursuit of service while stimulating my desire to create a supportive community and build coalitions.

Turning vision into action through leadership. I was recruited by B-W to energize and rejuvenate a program that, at one time, had served as a model of innovation and quality for adult learning. But more recently, the program had experienced a steady decline in enrollment and vitality—especially during the past ten years. My mandate is to create dynamic, innovative systems and generate a sense of confidence among LL constituents by responding to their needs while sustaining the high quality and reputation of the institution. Specifically, my highest priority is to actualize that portion of the first principle in the new B-W Strategic Plan that reads, "Baldwin-Wallace will remain . . . dedicated to excellence in all its educational programs for its undergraduate and graduate students" even when it means that reacquiring our maximum enrollment might take longer. But since a considerable portion of my vision requires me to serve as a change agent, an important feature of my task is to assist others through support, good communication, and a sense of shared partnership in our commitment to excellence and growth. While I strive to achieve and sustain innovative changes, part of my challenge is to build consensus, even when colleagues might initially be somewhat resistant.

Maintaining balance between the competing needs of adult students and the concerns expressed by the faculty. When dealing with adult learners, there seems to be a natural philosophical tension between the students and some faculty members. For these learners, there is a profound sense of urgency to complete their degree as quickly as possible. They tend to be highly pragmatic in their approach to degree completion. However, faculty members typically express their concerns regarding their desire to maintain the highest standards and practices in the classroom. They tend to see themselves as the primary gatekeepers and guardians of the curriculum and opposed to the students' position. But these competing expectations need not be mutually exclusive nor should they be perceived as incompatible. In the best practices of almost any field, successful leaders manage to align competing perspectives so that all stakeholders feel like their needs are met. My challenge, therefore, is to assist each group to understand and respect the other's perspective even while LL strives to achieve mutually beneficial resolutions. My strategy is to never sacrifice quality but always seek creative solutions to support adult learner needs. Since these issues are never fully resolved, I face an ongoing process that requires flexibility, sound problem solving skills, strong communication skills, wisdom, patience, a healthy dose of humility, and frequently, a sense of humor.

Administrative Methods, Strategies, Objectives

Methods. Wherever possible, I seek to empower others and assist all constituents to achieve their full potential. I strive to articulate my vision clearly but frame it in a manner that utilizes flexibility and the input of others so that it becomes a shared vision with everyone's ownership. Because LL serves such a broad constituency, I try to be sensitive and responsive to the needs of everyone we serve. Therefore, the primary methods I employ offer shared ownership to all stakeholders while I seek to create win/win situations.

Strategies. The strategies I use to accomplish these methods include the application of active listening skills, the willingness to subvert my ego, openness to criticism and feedback, and the ability to find humor in almost every situation. At the root of these strategies is a commitment to flexibility and the capacity to change according to whatever circumstances may define the situation so long as my standards are not compromised.

Objectives. I tend to operate from a parallel set of objectives: The first is for the division and the second (which flows from the first) is at a more personal level. At LL's second annual strategic planning retreat, the staff reiterated the mandate I was given when selected for this position: to recapture (or exceed) our previous maximum enrollment without in any way diluting the quality of our programs. During that retreat, LL determined that a multifaceted approach supported by a commitment to world-class courtesy would help define our strategy. As a result, we have employed the following scales to determine the rate of our success: 1) a weekly monitoring of admission activity (with a net increase of 24% enrollment during the most recent semester); 2) the ongoing development of initiatives that respond to student needs as articulated in the constant feedback segment of Administrative Responsibilities above (recent examples include the expansion to degree completion at our satellite campus—BWE, the development of an on-site introductory certificate called the "Gateway" specifically designed for classified staff in school districts, and, with the cooperation of the Education Division, the introduction of adult-friendly schedules for adult education majors); 3) being cited as a national benchmark by one or more national organizations dedicated to adult learning as evidenced by the various papers and presentations at recent conferences; and 4) being recognized by editors or researchers writing about adults and other lifelong learners that what we are doing at B-W is notable and a good example for others to imitate.

We identified a number of categories we seek to improve incrementally though we already believe the program is fundamentally sound: 1) In responding to the needs of everyone we serve, we strive to improve through the practice of world-class courtesy; 2) in course registration, we are refining our scheduling with a zero-cancellation target; 3) for curriculum-related issues, we are focusing on two aspects—better faculty development and support even as we continue to introduce a greater array of course delivery formats and options; 4) with BWE, our satellite campus, we are introducing a whole new dimension through degree completion and other initiatives designed to better respond to our constituents' needs from that location; and 5) through steady growth, we look to expand the number and kinds of students we can assist, regardless of whether their needs are for-credit or not-for-credit.

At a personal level, I want to see adult students fully integrated into the fabric of the B-W community. Nationally, many adult learners form a near-invisible group on campuses where they tend to be marginalized. They attend classes but are otherwise largely ignored in almost every aspect of campus life. In some instances, they tend to be unappreciated or even resented. My personal goal is to see the full integration of all learners on the campus—a goal that I believe is attainable since B-W already does a number of positive things in this regard that differ from less effective practices on many campuses.

I consider myself especially fortunate that B-W is a generous community and one of the very first colleges in the state of Ohio to welcome adult learners in 1947. The college has stronger administrative support and vision for adult and lifelong learners than almost every institution I have encountered. But what I envision is a sea change that will alter how the campus functions regarding the adult population it serves. In a nation that is on the brink of having more than 50% of total college enrollment 25 years of age or older, there need to be some significant changes in thinking about whom we serve and how we serve them. Therefore, my objective is to influence the B-W culture so that both faculty and learners can more fully explore and experience the full potential of what a learning community can become. And I hope to accomplish this in a manner that celebrates the presence of every learner on the campus.

Multisource Performance Evaluation Data

Lifelong Learning Advisory Council. Last year, at the conclusion of my first year at B-W, I sought an evaluation of my overall effectiveness from the members of the LL Advisory Council, comprised of one faculty member from each of the seven divisions and one at-large adjunct faculty member. Since this group has been consistently supportive (even enthusiastic) and positive in their feedback, I specifically requested that they make critical recommendations on how I could improve my effectiveness. They encouraged me to address three objectives they had identified: 1) Be prepared to offer concrete statistics and not appear to over-sell new initiatives when interacting with the faculty; 2) help create a more uniform approach to interacting with adjunct faculty, particularly through the better use of evaluations; and 3) increase communications regarding how LL is approaching certificates in contrast to degrees for adult learners.

Unsolicited feedback. I offer samples of responses I have received concerning a wide range of topics and initiatives. All original documentation is available upon request.

- **Student letters of appreciation.** "Thank you for making my beginning college experience so enjoyable! Your kindness, gentle criticism, patience, and gentle nudging made learning from you a pleasure. This was a valuable addition to my education autobiography." (card from Transformation class student, March 2001) "The individual care and timeliness with which you assisted me only strengthened the personal connection I have with B-W. Thank you again for caring about me, for I am certain that exact care is shared with each student you attend to." (card from student, January 2001) "Thank you for the new design of the evening and weekend course schedule for spring 2001! My friends and fellow students are very excited about it. This schedule is the most useful one I've ever seen. The information on every page is helpful and clearly written, and the format is easy to read. For the first time I can plan when I will graduate (the end of 2001) instead of waiting to discover which classes are offered each new semester. (email from student, November 2000)

- **Faculty and administrative responses to initiatives.** "What a great idea to bring Dr. Laura Palmer Noone to B-W to talk about the University of Phoenix! She generated some great ideas for us to consider, and the campus response I've heard has been excellent. Please keep the creative thought flowing and know you have support from the Division of Student Affairs." (memo from vice president for student affairs, October 2000) [In reaction to the publication of *Teaching Moments & Tips.*] "I think this was a wonderfully creative idea and had excellent results." (note from associate dean of student affairs, March 2000) "I wanted to say thanks for the notification of course payment memo I received from you recently. I had indeed been confused about the payment schedule, and the notice was very convenient; the idea of sending one every time would be just terrific. But more than that, I was mindful of your thoughtfulness. I was one of the faculty who had put in a query about the schedule, and the notice made me feel that somebody cared enough to respond, and to respond quickly. That's not always the case in this world, and I wanted you to know that I don't take it for granted. Thanks!" (memo from English department faculty member, March 2000)

Self-assessment. In terms of my tenure at B-W, I believe I have demonstrated the following strengths: 1) creativity and innovation—

This is an area in which I have probably exceeded all expectations; 2) project completion—For me, this is an item of equal importance, since I believe having good ideas isn't productive if you can't activate them, and I have been very successful in this area as well; 3) shared vision—is notable in its ripple effect as a wave of influence transforms a growing portion of the community, something I have been fortunate to sustain; and 4) sense of service—I see my role as a facilitator and strive to consistently serve the needs of the community, an area that probably gives me the greatest satisfaction.

In the following areas, I believe I have demonstrated moderate success but still need to improve: 1) engaging the campus in dialogue about adult learners—Through the LL Advisory Council, we have sought to engage faculty in a series of informal sessions to develop this discussion, but so far, we have not been able to make a significant impact; 2) promoting a collaborative relationship between LL and infrastructure support groups—Although colleagues have always been supportive, I sometimes have difficulty adjusting to internal processes and expectations, though I am improving; and 3) providing faculty development—This may be the single area on campus that needs more intentional intervention than any other, especially with adjuncts who are primarily my responsibility, but I have not created a system yet that will fully engage the faculty.

Five Most Significant Administrative Accomplishments

1. Bringing a sense of unity, accomplishment, and positive esteem to a division that had been perceived negatively for many years before I came to this position as reflected by numerous and ongoing comments ranging from the LL staff to members of the LL Advisory Council, the Undergraduate Curriculum Committee, and adjunct faculty.

2. Helping to stop the bleeding in regards to the steady enrollment decline among adult learners through multiple initiatives and interventions (with a net increase of more than 20% among newly admitted students for the most recent term).

3. Creating and implementing many unique and distinctive programs, formats, and courses including: The Gateway Certificate, The Century Program, the immersion format, and the transformation course. These initiatives have enabled LL to consistently remain at

the front of change on this campus while drawing increasingly positive media attention to the division and B-W (see Appendix C).

4. Publishing semester schedules, a strategic plan, the adult student handbook, and other documents that promote better communication and a heightened awareness of how the division functions within the institutional mission. The overall effect has been greater visibility and inclusion for LL.

5. The growth of not-for-credit learning experiences on campus. When I came to B-W, ILR had a membership of approximately 250—today that total exceeds 550 and continues to climb. We also opened a new ILR at BWE where, in the first year, enrollment has exceeded the third year enrollment of the same program on this campus. When coupled with our new Century Program, I believe B-W will become a national leader in how it integrates this significant portion of the population into learning opportunities on campus.

Areas for Improvement

I consider myself doubly fortunate to serve at an institution where high quality is the standard among so many top administrators and to have sufficient background from other schools that I can fully recognize the rare opportunity I am afforded by the model administrators I encounter here on a daily basis. The areas that need my primary attention seem to fall under three main categories: interacting with people, maximizing efficiency, and maintaining a positive perspective.

Interacting with people. Although I fully subscribe to the need for building relationships and strengthening communication with my colleagues, I sometimes feel like I have a built-in comfort zone in my office area so that I need to make a greater effort to mingle, build bridges, and generally improve that portion of consensus-building that is ultimately critical for success. Another aspect of this problem is the need for me to reinforce, in multiple dimensions, all the new initiatives we are generating as a division. I have found that for new initiatives to have full, unrestricted support I must constantly reinforce both the vision and action items among our support partners.

Maximizing efficiency. In this category, there are three strategies that continue to challenge me: 1) I do not always delegate duties and tasks that others could just as easily perform; in meetings and presentations, 2) I am sometimes inefficient in how I manage time; and 3) I don't always set aside time specifically for stress management and reduction.

Maintaining a positive perspective. I have often observed that the best leaders are always able to frame events and individuals within positive points-of-view. This is an area I hope to further develop since I believe it will be more likely to influence others when I seek their support and assistance.

Appendices
   A. Speeches & Presentations
   B. Internal Publications
   C. New Curricular Initiatives
   D. New Majors, Certificates, Programs, and Outreach Efforts
   E. Evaluation, Feedback, and Assessment
   F. Non-Credit Programs
   G. Active Role at National Conferences
   H. Committees

Lee Bash has served as Dean of the Division of Lifelong Learning at Baldwin-Wallace College since 1999.

ADMINISTRATIVE PORTFOLIO
Catherine Jarjisian
Director, Conservatory of Music
Baldwin-Wallace College
March 2001

Table of Contents

Introduction and Context
The purpose of this portfolio is to document and explicate my roles and responsibilities as Director of the Conservatory of Music at Baldwin-Wallace College. Designed to initiate both a formative process and a summative evaluation of my work for purposes of administrative review and personnel decisions, this portfolio also offers a valuable opportunity for personal reflection and for growth as an administrator.

Baldwin-Wallace College. An independent, coeducational, Methodist-affiliated institution, Baldwin-Wallace is located in a suburban city southwest of Cleveland. The college serves a total of almost 5,000 students; 2,600 of those have full-time, undergraduate status. Committed to the comprehensive education of undergraduate students with the liberal arts and sciences as a basis, Baldwin-Wallace also offers professional programs in business, education, and music as well as graduate degrees in business and education.

The Conservatory of Music. One of seven academic divisions of the college, the conservatory is a professional school of music that offers to selected students preparation for careers as performers, educators, scholars, therapists, and/or arts administrators. Instruction is provided as well to students wishing to study music as a liberal art. With applied study available in all standard orchestral instruments plus guitar, keyboard, and voice, the conservatory also provides 14 student ensembles, some of which include college students, faculty and staff, and community members.

The Music Division comprises seven departments, one consortial program, the Jones Music Library, the Riemenschneider Bach Institute, and the Preparatory/Adult Education Department. At present, there are 242 conservatory students and 1,400 preparatory and adult education students who receive instruction late in the day and on weekends. (The conservatory's structure is shown in Appendix A.)

Administrative Responsibilities
The duties of the Conservatory Director fall into four broad categories. (See Appendix B for a table showing approximate time allocations for tasks involved in each.)

Educational leadership. I am charged with developing a vision and guiding efforts toward realizing the conservatory's mission, goals, and objectives. I also oversee curricular development and revision and establish the overall administrative structure. I lead and respond to initiatives from on- and off-campus to augment or modify program offerings, especially for nontraditional student populations. Finally, I supervise particular functions (e.g., concert production, touring) typifying professional education in music.

Personnel. Currently there are 58 full-time and adjunct members of the teaching faculty, 23 administrative and academic support staff members, and 101 employees serving the Music Therapy Consortium and the Preparatory and Adult Education Department. (See Appendix C for a list of conservatory personnel.) I have responsibility for hiring and developing, supervising, and evaluating all conservatory faculty and staff members as well a large number of student workers, many of whom perform staff functions such as concert recording, stage management, and clerical work.

In the role of mentor to faculty members, I meet at least three times yearly with each non-tenured faculty members and write a report of my teaching observations and our discussions. Additional conferences are scheduled to discuss planned tenure or promotion applications. In my supervisory and evaluative capacity, I undertake steps as necessary to improve the quality of teaching or to remove ineffective teachers. I also conduct the annual reviews of non-tenured faculty members according to procedures I drafted for faculty approval last year (see Appendix D); chair individual review committees for pre-tenured faculty members; and make recommendations for tenure and promotion.

Resource management. As part of my responsibility for facilities, instruments and equipment, and financial resources, I make annual requests in three categories (information technology, capital, operating) for conservatory resources and monitor two general (instructional, administrative) accounts and several specialized accounts (Preparatory/Adult Education, Riemenschneider Bach Institute, Music Therapy, Summer Programs). I also oversee endowed accounts for particular purposes (e.g., instrument repair and guest artists), and select recipients of named scholarships for enrolled music students as well as talent-based awards for entering students. (See Appendix E for a list of conservatory budgets and accounts as well as total budgetary allotments.)

External relationships. Among my regular interactions with a number of constituencies both on- and off-campus, I participate in the admission process by undertaking recruiting travel, speaking to parents on audition days and with prospective students and parents on visitation days, and making final admission and talent award decisions for the conservatory. I host and visit with alumni and donors and communicate both formally and informally with many. I also coordinate special events like the Bach and Focus Festivals and direct summer programs.

Philosophy of Administrative Practice

I believe myself to be effective as an administrator to the extent that three essential components are in constant evidence: energetic, visionary leadership; support, encouragement, and sometime prodding of faculty as autonomous, but collaborative educational experts; and a facilitating, serving presence among capable, even gifted, colleagues. This three-pronged image suggests that I am at once, or alternately, out in front, pushing from behind, and walking beside.

Administrative Objectives and Methods

Objectives. My current aims as Conservatory Director are several:

1. Hire and/or develop an outstanding faculty and staff.

2. Support faculty and student achievements, including performance and scholarly activity.

3. Ensure a balanced enrollment of highly selective students representing diverse cultures, backgrounds, and aspirations.

4. Improve the interdependence between the conservatory and the college.

5. Enhance the conservatory's visibility and outreach into the broader community.

6. Pursue my own professional development as an administrator.

Methods. To achieve these objectives, I have sought to:

1. A. Refine the conservatory's structure and operations, including developing, reviving, and/or revitalizing governance bodies, search procedures, promotion and tenure guidelines, policies for daily or regular activity of staff members, and expectations for faculty and staff roles in carrying out the conservatory's mission (see Appendix F for draft of revised mission statement, goals, and conservatory-wide objectives).

B. Communicate continually, both formally and informally, with faculty and staff. (See Appendix G for examples of letters, addresses, and reports.)

2. A. Attend most conservatory performances as well as important off-campus performances (e.g., Cleveland Opera, Cain Park, Blossom) featuring Baldwin-Wallace faculty or students. (See Appendix H for list of on-campus conservatory performances.)

B. Encourage and approve expenditures for a wide variety of faculty development activities.

3. A. Represent Baldwin-Wallace at college fairs and state conferences and travel domestically and internationally to record auditions and recruit students.

B. Make admission decisions and target talent-based awards to students most likely to benefit from and contribute to the conservatory's comprehensive educational program.

C. Within existing constraints, upgrade the quality of the physical environment in which students and faculty are seeking to work. Among other efforts, this has included a major lighting and sound upgrade in the concert hall and minor renovation (dividing office spaces).

4. A. Revise operational procedures (e.g., scholarship awarding) to align more closely with procedures followed in other divisions.

B. Take advantage of opportunities to educate conservatory faculty about college ways and vice versa. Meet regularly with directors and deans about college-wide issues.

C. Foster connections between conservatory and college faculty members, especially toward collaborative educational ventures. Encourage active conservatory faculty participation in general faculty governance.

5. A. Undertake significant efforts to meet alumni and cultivate donors, both current and potential.

B. Make public appearances and presentations as requested, desirable, or necessary.

C. Participate actively as a performer, both as a regular chorister and as an occasional alto soloist for performances on campus or in Cleveland.

D. Serve in leadership capacities in professional organizations such as the National Association of Schools of Music and the Ohio Association of Music Schools (see Curriculum Vitae, Appendix I).

6. Seek personal administrative development opportunities such as attending MLE (Harvard, 1999), workshops on fundraising (1999), and futures planning (2000) sponsored by the National Association of Schools of Music, and the Kansas State University conference for Academic Chairpersons (2001). (See Appendix J for a list of conferences and meetings attended.)

Performance Evaluation

Self-assessment. During the spring of 1999, I evaluated my first year's work at Baldwin-Wallace in a report to the dean (Appendix K), according to five goals I had set for the year that in turn were derived from two directives presented to me by the president. He charged me to develop a vision for the conservatory's future and to increase the conservatory's outreach, both across campus and into the community.

During the second year, I chose to build on my previous work and add three goals, these informed in part by my participation in Harvard's MLE Institute during the summer of 1999. I solicited the conservatory faculty's assessment of my work, asking them to comment briefly on progress toward both the goals I had derived and those made clear to me by faculty members during my interview and in the first months of my tenure, and I included in my annual report for that year (Appendix L) a summary of the feedback provided by faculty members. I noted that conservatory faculty and staff perceived that work was "proceeding more or less satisfactorily on tasks reflecting the goals as stated," and I made additional observations about a general but probably appropriate lack of awareness of the director's outside work; the impact of the college's present academic and administrative structure on the ability of the conservatory to integrate more fully into campus life; the elusiveness of the goal of students' empowerment over their own learning; and the need for help in upgrading the quality of instruction. Again, I added three goals for the new year (2000-01), these having to do with fostering collegial interactions; revising the conservatory's mission statement, goals, and objectives; and beginning work on a conservatory-wide assessment plan.

My own assessment points to opportunities for growth. In particular, I find part of my administrative philosophy to be elusive in practice, that is the belief in an autonomous, yet collaborative faculty functioning on the basis of individual and collective educational expertise. I have been surprised and occasionally dismayed with colleagues' reluctance to engage in challenges and risks even with the hope of widespread benefit. I suspect that students' unwillingness to assume ownership of their own learning is related and provides a second opportunity for growth. Finally, I need to encourage interaction within the conservatory community, in part to foster increased autonomy and collaboration.

Dean's assessment. In the spring of 1999, the dean expressed complete satisfaction with my work ("I simply cannot imagine any way in which it could have been better than it was") and invited me to share with faculty and staff my vision for the conservatory's short-term (five years) future. I chose to do that the following August in an address to conservatory faculty and staff ("Let There Be Light"), which the dean attended and which is included in Appendix G.

Others' assessment. Appendix M contains copies of unsolicited cards and letters from students, faculty members, campus colleagues, and external colleagues and friends of the college.

Most Significant Administrative Accomplishments

1. Hiring and developing several new and replacement faculty and staff members and admitting higher-ability students. We have conducted searches for and hired seven full-time faculty members; all have contributed significantly to the conservatory's education program. We have received new positions for staff (custodian, music librarian), and expansions of others (assistant director, outreach director). We also have hired adjunct faculty members and staff accompanists on the basis of actual (simplified) searches, a change in practice for the conservatory. Finally, we have begun to compete at a higher level for students (see Appendix N for cross-application data).

2. Successful cultivation of development potential leading to significant foundation support and new/increased named-scholarship accounts and a concomitant responsible approach to budgetary monitoring. We have been funded three times by the Kulas Foundation: $200,000 for the concert hall lighting project, $16,000 for a new string bass, and $50,000 toward the purchase of a German Steinway piano. (See Appendix O for records of conservatory gifts, 1998–2000.) We also have reduced the $250,000 financial aid deficit (Griffiths funds), eliminated waste in student wage expenditures, conducted strict oversight

of adjunct faculty loads and compensation, and kept detailed records of expenses and encumbrances.

3. Formation of a conservatory advisory board of professional musicians from a variety of fields (see Appendix P) to offer guidance in meeting conservatory goals. Members include prominent conductors and directors, writers, and the president of Cleveland's classical music radio station.

4. Invitation to travel with representatives of Oberlin College, the Peabody Conservatory, and the University of Miami on an annual five-city (Tokyo, Seoul, Taipei, Hong Kong, Singapore) tour to record auditions of prospective students and participate in university fairs. Baldwin-Wallace can take advantage of the 12-year work of three well-known music schools, thereby shortening the time it will take to develop a stream of students from Asia to the conservatory.

5. Renewal of National Association of Schools of Music (NASM) accreditation. It became necessary during my first semester at Baldwin-Wallace to rewrite and write a self-study for the upcoming accreditation review by the National Association of Schools of Music. With the assistance of others, I authored the self-study, then shepherded the conservatory and college successfully through the review process. Our reaccreditation was approved for the maximum period of ten years. (See Appendix Q for a copy of the NASM visitors' report.)

For additional detail about conservatory operations and activities, please consult the divisional reports from 1998–99 and 1999–2000 found in Appendix R.

Administrative and Professional Contributions and Recognition
(See Appendix S for a complete listing.)

National. As the official institutional representative to the National Association of Schools of Music, I have attended yearly conferences and special professional development workshops and recently have begun serving as a visiting evaluator on NASM accreditation teams. I also am a new member of NASM's ethics committee. During the past year I was cited in a compiled directory of significant women in music during the 20th century, selected to receive the Certificate of Honor by the Esther Boyer College of Music Alumni Association of Temple University, and invited to serve on a panel of visionary deans at the Conference of the American Orff-Schulwerk Association in Rochester, NY.

State and regional. Currently I am president-elect of the Ohio Association of Music Schools and NASM Region Five secretary. In 1998-1999, I served on the Arts Writing Panel of the Joint Council of the Council for Basic Education and the Ohio Board of Regents.

Campus. Although not eligible to serve on committees of the general faculty, I was elected to the search committee for the vice president for academic affairs.

Administrative Goals

Short-term. During the next one-to-three years, I intend to:

1. Address the balance of full-time and part-time faculty in three conservatory departments: keyboard, music theory and history and literature, and voice.

2. Upgrade the pedagogical support environment through additions and enhancements to conservatory audio, video, and computing capabilities.

3. Develop and cultivate a more significant relationship with preparatory/adult education department parents and alumni.

4. Revise the conservatory mission statement, goals, and conservatory-wide objectives. Oversee the revision of department/program objectives.

5. Develop sophomore comprehensive reviews in all majors.

6. Improve marketing efforts, especially the web page.

7. Develop a long-term plan for recruiting that makes use of faculty performance and master classes, ensemble touring, and on-campus opportunities for school-age learners and teachers.

8. Develop and/or cultivate relationships with top donor prospects and with conservatory alumni in general.

Long-term. Over a longer period and in more general terms, I intend to:

1. Develop a balanced (major and applied area), diverse, and selective student body.

2. Foster a diverse, vital, and professionally engaged faculty.

3. Develop ongoing, division-wide review and accountability procedures tied to conservatory and college missions, goals, and objectives.

4. Establish the conservatory as the musical presence on Cleveland's west side.

5. Increase outside financial support of students and programs.

6. Renovate and expand facilities to provide an environment worthy of the conservatory's educational programs.

Appendices

A. Conservatory Structure

B. Table of Time Allotments for Director's Tasks

C. Conservatory Personnel

D. Conservatory Promotion and Tenure Guidelines

E. Conservatory Budgets and Accounts

F. Conservatory Mission, Goals, Objectives

G. Letters, Addresses, Reports

H. On-campus Conservatory Performances

I. Curriculum Vitae

J. Conferences/meetings Attended

K. Annual Report and Dean's Evaluation, 1998-99

L. Annual Report, 1999-00

M. Unsolicited Evaluations

N. Cross-application Data

O. Conservatory Gifts, 1998-2000

P. Conservatory Advisory Board

Catherine Jarjisian is Director of the Conservatory of Music and Chair, Music Division, at Baldwin-Wallace College.

ADMINISTRATIVE PORTFOLIO FOR IMPROVEMENT
G. Andrew Mickley
Chair, Department of Psychology
Baldwin-Wallace College
March 2001

Table of Contents

Introduction

Purpose of this portfolio. The purpose of this portfolio is to document my responsibilities, achievements, methods, and goals as I serve as chair of the Department of Psychology at Baldwin-Wallace College

(B-W). Ultimately, I hope to have a better remembrance of what has transpired in the five years that I have been department chair and how I might build on this experience to make my remaining time as chair a period of effective leadership. The goals of my leadership include, foremost, providing a quality education for the students who study psychology at B-W. Instrumental in achieving this goal is the necessity of developing a strong, committed, faculty and providing them the resources they need to do their job.

Institutional context. The Psychology Department is part of the Social Sciences Division which includes the departments of Economics, Political Science, and Sociology. B-W is an independent, coeducational college founded in the liberal arts tradition in 1845 in Berea, Ohio, a suburb of southwest Cleveland. Today the college serves approximately 4,800 students, including 2,600 full-time undergraduates, 1,550 part-time students, and 650 graduate students in business administration and education.

Department of Psychology. The chair of the Psychology Department is elected by his/her departmental peers, appointed by the academic dean and serves a three-year term. Reelection is possible. There are ten full-time faculty in the Department of Psychology, and we serve approximately 230 majors. Psychology is a popular elective as students select courses to meet core requirements and so almost all of the 4,800 students at B-W take one or more of our courses during their undergraduate career. Our department recently proposed and implemented an interdisciplinary major in neuroscience which was offered for the first time last year. We are in the process of developing a masters program in community psychology. The faculty of the Psychology Department come from diverse backgrounds, and their training represents all of the major sub-areas of the discipline. We are a dedicated, hard-working group who are passionate about psychology and our profession. This passion extends beyond the department as all of our faculty are also leaders involved in numerous campus committees and college-wide initiatives.

Statement of Administrative Responsibilities
Personnel management of office staff

- Supervise quality of secretary's work.

- Assign department tasks to secretary.

- Address special needs/problems of staff.

- Monitor workload and changes in departmental staffing needs.
- Coordinate hiring of student office assistants with secretary.
- Coordinate supervision of students with secretary.
- Manage special needs/problems.
- Hire and supervise student office help in summer or during other absences of secretary.

Faculty support (full- and part-time)

- Evaluate short-term and long-term need.
- Formally request hiring of new faculty.
- Supervise search for new faculty.
- Orient and mentor new faculty.
- Coordinate all faculty reviews: annual, expanded second and fourth year reviews, promotion, tenure.
- Write evaluation letters for all faculty reviews.
- Advocate and encourage faculty professional development.
- Evaluate and write recommendation letters on all requests for sabbatical and/or other leaves.
- Evaluate special requests for leaves or change in status.
- Manage complaints by and about faculty.
- Complete overload report for Registrar's Office.
- Communicate with part-time faculty regarding quality of teaching and their integration into the department.
- Maintain communication and cooperation with Life Long Learning (LLL) office regarding part-time faculty.
- Maintain liaison with college relations to promote accomplishments and expertise of both full- and part-time faculty.

Student support

- Receive, evaluate, and resolve complaints.
- Develop and implement conflict resolution strategies.
- Evaluate transfer credit requests.

- Evaluate requests for special exceptions including course waivers and substitutions.

- Initiate and supervise efforts to recruit new students into the major or minor.

- Supervise the creation and maintenance of the department web site.

- Distribute advisees to faculty and ensure quality advising within department.

- Organize and supervise selection of Honors Day recipients.

- Organize and supervise department's efforts to maintain alumni relations.

- Advise clubs/honor societies or ensure that other faculty are handling this responsibility.

- Assign faculty advisors and coordinate advisement activities with campus academic advising office.

- Develop internship opportunities for students and serve as liaison with career services and external community.

- Take phone calls from parents; resolve problems.

Curricular issues—short-term

- Work with dean's office, LLL, and registrar's office to plan the annual course schedule.

- Adjust the schedule and coordinate any change with registrar's office, LLL, bookstore, and dean's office.

- Write annual department assessment report.

- Write all requests for changes in course requirements, new courses, or any other curricular matters.

Curricular issues—long-term

- Initiate discussions of new course offerings.

- Initiate discussions of course content and pedagogy.

- Supervise department's assessment efforts and implementation of feedback steps.

- Initiate and follow up on creation of new majors, minors, or inter-disciplinary programs.

Budgeting/facilities management

- Assess short- and long-term needs for supplies and furniture/equipment.

- Assess short- and long-term computer hardware and software needs.

- Assess short- and long-term needs regarding space utilization/renovation/remodeling.

- Write annual budget request.

- Write annual capital budget request.

- Write annual computer capital budget request.

- Supervise all renovations, remodeling or reorganizing of departmental space.

Communications

- Write annual departmental report.

- Write annual assessment report.

- Participate in meetings of department chairs called by dean.

- Organize regular department meetings.

- Organize annual department retreats.

Table 1
Approximate Percentage of Time Engaged
in Each Department Chair Function

Chair Function	Percent Time
Staff Management	5%
Faculty support	25%
Student Support	25%
Curricular Issues	20%
Budgeting/Facilities management	10%
Communications	15%

- Represent department, when requested, at meetings of trustees or other college functions.

- Represent department to external community including the media, employers, graduate schools.

Reflective Statement of Administrative Philosophy, Methodology, and Objectives

I am an optimistic, people-focused and people-confident leader. My administrative philosophy has as its foundation the strong belief that the students, faculty, and administrative staff with whom I serve, are good, strong, hard-working people. They are individuals who are passionately interested in learning, pedagogy, college service, and scholarship. They do not need to be coerced into doing a superior job within their profession. What in large part determines their ability to be at the top of their game is the organizational environment and systems in which they work. For practical reasons such as the limitations of money, space, time, training, and experience, individuals or teams are usually not achieving their potential. It is my privilege as department chair to work with each of my constituencies to develop the resources and organizational systems that will enable us to thrive. In one sense I act as a jungle guide, hacking away at the underbrush, so that my colleagues and I may have a smoother path on which to tread as we move toward our goals. Of course, the person out front hopefully knows where he is going, has a vision of the final destination, and provides a model that others might choose to follow. This is the nature of my work as department chair.

If circumstances were different, how would I like to be treated by my department chair? This is the guiding principle that I use as I go about my responsibilities. As department chair, I am both a faculty colleague and supervisor. I am not a permanent chair. When my time as chair ends, I may continue doing administrative things at a different level or I may be back in the trenches. While in this role, my goal is to model respectful, collegial, and service-oriented leadership.

My methods of leadership and management are always democratic although my decision-making cannot always follow this path. Specifically, I seek wide input from all my constituencies and do what I can to encourage consensus building. Developing consensus is far and away the best outcome because it promotes ownership of the final decision and makes compliance more likely. I believe I have done my job well if I have facilitated a democratic decision (see Appendix A for a typical Psychology Department Meeting Agenda and Appendix B for an Annual Report of the Psychology Department).

Still, there are some decisions that are either trivial (and therefore no one really wants to be involved) or sufficiently contentious that consensus is unlikely. The trivial decisions are easily handled. I resolve the contentious decisions by soliciting extensive advice from each constituent and then achieving consensus on how the final decision should be made. Sometimes I am the logical decision-maker, but sometimes a person in a different office is best consulted. An important aspect of leadership is knowing which person to consult and which decision requires which method of resolution.

Services and Programs Offered to Colleagues
I offer a variety of opportunities for growth and development to members of the Department of Psychology as well as to my department chair colleagues at B-W. Our departmental history is one in which faculty have rarely applied for external research support. In an attempt to change this pattern, I offer symposia on how to attract outside funding for research. This involves asking managers from the development office to speak to our group. I also provide resources concerning funding sources and methods. (See Appendix C for an example of a Council on Undergraduate Research (CUR) grant writing workshop that I promoted at B-W.)

Our faculty members are always too busy, and this means that we usually deal with the urgent portions of our calendars but all too often have little time for reflection and discussion about important topics. Each semester I coordinate a series of informal forums in which faculty can come and share their joys and concerns about teaching and ongoing research. Not only are the sessions therapeutic, but they also frequently publicize useful pedagogical hints and spawn research collaboration. (See Appendix D for a typical semester schedule of such meetings.)

Our department has a large number of part-time faculty, and it is a challenge to give them a sense of involvement and keep the full-time faculty informed about their adjunct colleagues. Each semester we have at least one joint full-time/adjunct faculty meeting. There is an important social/communicative component to this meeting. Beyond this, however, the topical agenda is driven primarily by our adjunct faculty and is designed to meet their needs. (See Appendix E for an agenda from one of these Adjunct/Full-time faculty meetings.)

When I became chair five years ago, there was no real forum that would allow me to talk with a group of other department chairs, to build bridges, share useful methods of leadership, or to learn from my peers. Three years ago, I motivated a series of monthly department chair lunches. These are informal meetings, supported by the academic dean's office, in which we discuss an administrative/academic topic generated by one of us. Mostly, however, it is a place to network, facilitate communication, and informally build administrative skills. (See Appendix F for an announcement of one of these department chair meetings.)

Steps Taken to Develop as an Academic Administrator
My goals for professional development have been facilitated by courses and independent reading. Each year I have sought to receive formal training in my administrative work. In 1997, I attended an American Council on Education (ACE) seminar on chairing the academic department. Since many of my interests lie in encouraging faculty development and in developing systems to facilitate student-faculty collaboration in research, some of these seminars and workshops have involved working with the Council on Undergraduate Research (CUR) and Project Kaleidoscope (PKAL). This year, in a national election, I was selected to be a CUR counselor and serve on the board. I am also an avid reader of administrative books and journals including, for example, Allan Tucker, *Chairing the Academic Department,* ACE/Macmillan, 1992; John B. Bennett & David J. Figuli, *Enhancing Departmental Leadership: The Roles of the Chairperson,* ACE/Macmillan, 1990; Mary Lou Higgerson, *Communication Skills for Department Chairs,* Anker, 1996; Irene W. D. Hecht, Mary Lou Higgerson, Walter H. Gmelch, & Allan Tucker, *The Department Chair as Academic Leader,* Oryx, 1999; and *The Department Chair: A Resource for Academic Administrators,* Anker.

These workshops and other experiences have taught me that there are some aspects of administration for which I can muster little interest, while I can become passionate about other portions of my job as department chair. For example, as a result of a CUR conference on institutionalizing undergraduate research, I became a member of a task force that developed a proposal to facilitate student-faculty collaborative research projects at B-W. This plan outlined a method by which faculty can make research mentoring part of their normal workload, provided incentives for student-faculty research, and assisted faculty members in their quest for extramural grants. Similarly, a joint CUR/PKAL workshop enabled me to lead the B-W Faculty Development Committee as we developed a plan aimed at keeping post-tenure faculty vital. This plan is being pilot tested in the Psychology Department. (See Appendix G for an outline of this plan.)

Multisource Performance Evaluation
Many people who serve in the role of department chair have significant professorial and academic experience but little administrative experience. My history is not typical. I spent the first 21 years of my career as an officer in the United States Air Force (USAF) teaching in academic programs (at the USAF Academy and the Uniformed Services University of the Health Sciences), managing these programs and doing research. As compared to civilian academic programs, feedback on performance within the Department of Defense is constant and part of the system. Each year I was evaluated by supervisors and peers. My ability to administer programs was part of that evaluation.

This personal history provided me with a mindset that constant feedback is necessary for improvement. Thus, when I was elected department chair, I made a point of scheduling a yearly meeting with my immediate supervisor, the academic dean, to solicit advice on how I might improve my effectiveness in chairing the department. During the summers, I make appointments with each of the faculty members in my department to receive their assessment of my performance. I model within our department the idea that self-evaluation and continuous feedback is expected and appreciated.

Evaluation by psychology faculty and staff. Earlier this year I asked each faculty and staff member in the Psychology Department to provide comments on how I am doing as a department chair and colleague. I listed a number of specific areas in which I sought feedback and asked that they place their responses (without identifying marks) in my mailbox. The full results of this feedback are in Appendix H. Below are some of the dominant themes expressed.

- **Department planning:** Faculty perceive me as being on top of all the many details involved in short- and long-term planning for our department and having fostered growth within the department by negotiating for more lab space, computer upgrades, new programs and additional faculty.

- **Departmental decision-making:** Faculty perceive me as soliciting input from all concerned department members and making decisions after carefully considering all the facts and opinions.

- **Communication skills:** Faculty describe me as capable of expressing my thoughts in a non-confrontational manner, making others feel comfortable expressing themselves to me, and giving their point of view fair consideration.

- **Problem solving:** Faculty perceive me as being very good at analyzing a situation but also being open to creative solutions generated by others.

- **Resource management:** The faculty and staff report that they get what they need to do their jobs.

- **How is my teaching?:** Faculty perceive me as a rigorous and effective teacher.

- **How is my scholarly work?:** Faculty perceive me as the most active scholar in the department and credit me with folding students into the research process and keeping up with the students after they graduate.

- **How is my departmental/campus service?:** Faculty believe that I am very active and contribute significantly to the work of a variety of important B-W committees.

- **What is my strongest suit?:** Faculty and staff comment on my strong organizational skills and their perception that I serve as a model for students and for faculty alike, "showing discretion and consideration but also by being so active so that everyone wants to emulate" the way I do my work.

Evaluation by academic dean. Find, in Appendix I, verbatim comments reflecting recent feedback from the academic dean. The common themes expressed during this evaluation indicate that I excel in decision-making. I am perceived as especially strong in the areas of curricular, personnel, and facilities decisions. The academic dean appreciates how her office is kept in the information loop as department planning unfolds. My oral and written communication skills are evaluated as my strongest suit. In particular, the academic dean cites my ability to listen well even when others may be more emotional and less rational, my ability to make clear and well-structured presentations, and my ability to build consensus. The academic dean is also impressed by my research and appreciates my effort to secure external funds and to include undergraduate students in my scholarly work. My departmental and campus service was labeled as "Outstanding." Special note was taken of the time spent organizing chair lunches, CUR activities, and chairing the Social Sciences Division.

Self-evaluation: what's gone well? When I began as chair five years ago, there were eight full-time faculty members in the Psychology Department and over 20 adjunct faculty. We were (and continue to be) a popular major, but we were understaffed. This problem was exacerbated by the fact that our talented full-time faculty were contributing other places around campus (honors program, assessment) and received release time for their work elsewhere. This necessitated us using an inordinate number of adjunct faculty to teach our courses. At one point, over 60% of our courses were taught by part-time faculty. Since our adjunct faculty do not do academic advising or share responsibility for committee work or program management, this situation placed a significant strain on the full-time faculty. Perhaps more importantly, it also created a situation in which our psychology majors could go through their entire undergraduate academic career without having an opportunity to take a full-time faculty member's course. One of my successes as chair has been my ability to advocate for more full-time faculty for the Department of Psychology. This year we are hiring our 10th full-time faculty member. The number of adjunct faculty we now employ has decreased, and faculty morale is up. (See faculty comments in Chair Feedback, Appendix H.)

For as long as anyone can remember, the Department of Psychology has been housed in Carnegie Hall, a century-old building that looked it. Laboratory space was almost non-existent. Classrooms were dominated by water pipes and falling plaster. Faculty offices were quaint. Before I became chair, there was active advocacy for renovation of the building, and the college administration was supportive. During my tenure, a donor was identified, and it was left to me (and the chairs of the Departments of Sociology and Political Science) to work with the architects and our own construction supervisors to design the new space, coordinate transitional moves for the department, and equip the new facility. Anyone who has built a house will have an appreciation for the complexity of the $7.6 million, 46,000 square feet project which called for renovation of Carnegie Hall as well as an adjacent building and the construction of an annex connecting the two. This year we moved back to the renovated building and, by all accounts, it is a real success. Our students now have wonderful laboratory space in which to work. Classrooms are hospitable, and faculty offices are comfortable and conducive to our work.

The field of psychology has it roots in biology and philosophy, but modern psychology has gravitated more towards the sciences than the humanities. One of the reasons I was hired eight years ago was to move the department toward a closer affiliation with neuroscience (the study of the brain and behavior). During my time as chair, our department developed a neuroscience minor and an interdisciplinary major (with biology and chemistry). We built a new neuroscience laboratory. I wrote several grant proposals and attracted funding from the National Science Foundation (NSF) to equip our new laboratory (see Table 2 and further information in Appendix J). I also wrote an NSF Research in Undergraduate Institutions (RUI) grant that funded the student-faculty collaborative research conducted in the new lab. I continue to apply for extramural funding from the National Institutes of Health (NIH) to support neuroscience research involving undergraduate students as co-investigators. We now have a very active neuroscience program, and our students are going on to graduate programs in neuroscience and physiological psychology as well as becoming successful physicians and veterinarians. (See Appendix K for a list of students whom I mentored who are currently involved in, or have completed, post-graduate work.)

| Table 2 | | | |
| Extramural Grant Submissions and Funding | | | |
Year	Source	Amount Requested ($)	Amount Funded ($)
1994	NSF	38,956	34,663
1995	NSF	316,198	210,000
1997	NSF	12,000	6,000
1998	NSF	12,000	12,000
1999	NSF	5,000	5,000
2000	NSF	10,000	10,000
2001	NIH	100,000	Pending

Self-evaluation: What has not gone well? Our psychology faculty is comprised of seven tenured and three non-tenured members. Thus the majority of my colleagues are mid- or late-career. We have not done a good job in defining expectations for our post-tenure faculty. Nor have we allowed faculty to help shape what the latter stages of their career in academia will be like.

Part of this larger issue has to do with post-tenure feedback for faculty. I am a strong advocate of the tenure system as a means by which academic freedom may be preserved. But in our department (and in most other departments at Baldwin-Wallace) there is not an accepted means by which post-tenure faculty receive feedback on performance. Most of our post-tenure faculty continue to receive feedback on their teaching via the standard student questionnaires. But teaching feedback from other sources and feedback regarding the other aspects of a faculty member's workload is not routine.

Maintaining a reasonable, healthy faculty workload is another area that has not gone well during my years as chair. I am fortunate to have a highly motivated and talented psychology faculty. Unfortunately, I continually witness frantic colleagues working into the evenings and on weekends. We have had a number of conversations within our department regarding "What is a reasonable standard for commitment to the college?" "How should I balance my work and my private life?" While parts of these decisions involve personal choice and setting personal limits on what one can handle, they also involve institutional issues. The faculty workload at B-W is based only on teaching responsibilities, but evaluation for tenure and promotion also considers performance in scholarly work, college service, academic advising, and maintaining professional/ethical relationships. This leaves a fair amount of ambiguity regarding expectations outside the classroom. Thus, I do not believe that faculty workload has been sufficiently well-defined either in the Department of Psychology or at B-W.

Administrative Goals

1. I plan to develop a program for post-tenure faculty members of our department that will enable and encourage them to establish professional goals aimed at continuing faculty development (see proposal in Appendix G). The expectation is that, with cooperation of the college administration, we can design faculty development plans that will encourage faculty vitality while simultaneously promoting

institutional objectives. The program is to be in place for self-selected faculty members by the 2002-2003 academic year.

2. I plan to establish a system by which the faculty of the Department of Psychology design and embrace a method of more consistent performance feedback. The pilot program is to be in place by the 2003-2004 academic year. The large-scale program is to be in place by the 2004-2005 academic year.

3. In order to begin to address issues of faculty workload, I plan to explore the feasibility of performing a needs assessment within the Department of Psychology. This will involve a systematic look at what resources we need over the next five to ten years to do our jobs in an excellent way. Included in this assessment would be what we need in terms of faculty time. The feasibility is to be determined during the 2001-2002 academic year. Assessment is to be completed during the 2002-2003 academic year.

4. The Psychology Department has begun to explore the possibility of offering a Masters Degree (M.S.) in Community Psychology. Informal analysis of student interest in this program is encouraging. But a comprehensive quality proposal for this new program must include: a) a curriculum plan, b) identification of faculty to teach the courses, c) methods for recruitment of excellent students, d) an estimate regarding the employability of our future graduates, e) identification of sites and supervisors for internships and practicums, and f) identification of resources that we will need to begin this program.

Our department has identified a faculty member who is interested in directing the new masters program. However, this faculty member needs time to develop the proposal. I will advocate release time for this faculty member to develop a quality proposal on behalf of the department. The proposal will be completed by December 2001. The coordination/approval of the proposal will be completed by December 2002. The first class will begin in September 2003.

Appendices
A. Psychology Department Meeting Agenda
B. Psychology Department Annual Report
C. Council on Undergraduate Research (CUR) Grant Writing Workshop

D. Schedule of Teaching/Research Development Meetings for Psychology Faculty
E. Agenda for Psychology Adjunct/Full-time Faculty Meeting
F. Announcement of Department Chair Lunch Meetings to Facilitate Communication
G. Plan to Maintain Post-tenure Vitality of Psychology Faculty
H. Chair Performance Evaluations from Faculty and Staff
 I. Chair Performance Evaluations from Academic Dean

G. Andrew Mickley is Professor and Chair, Department of Psychology, Baldwin-Wallace College.

ADMINISTRATIVE PORTFOLIO
John Zubizarreta
Dean of Undergraduate Studies
Director of Honors and Faculty Development
Professor of English
Columbia College
Spring 2001

Table of Contents

Portfolio Preface and Rationale

For ten years, since I first developed a teaching portfolio, I have invested a considerable amount of my personal and professional energy to the virtue of reflective practice. My effort has been an endeavor that challenges teachers and scholars to improve their influence on students and the academy by continually examining the core principles and practices that distinguish the nature and efficacy of their work within a context of collaboration and peer review. Why should such rigorous analysis and accountability be confined to faculty? Administrators, too, should engage in the benefits of reflection and assessment for improvement, a process that also provides an authentic basis for valid evaluation of administrative performance.

This portfolio, then, has the twin purposes of both improvement and assessment for annual merit review of my dual responsibilities as dean and professor. It is an ongoing tool for strengthening my position as dean of undergraduate studies while also serving as a frame for my reflections about the tensions between serving in an administrative capacity and maintaining my vigorous commitment to teaching and scholarship.

The portfolio, therefore, contains a mix of information relevant to my unique situation as a dean with unbroken ties to the faculty role. In this sense, my portfolio has a distinct edge not typical of a full-time administrative dean's profile: It is the testy edge of a faculty member with a hand in administration.

Responsibilities
In summer 1998, I accepted an appointment to the position of dean of undergraduate studies, a post I insisted I would abandon immediately if it began to interfere consequentially with my passion for teaching, learning, and scholarship. Crazy, perhaps, but I felt I could find creative, fulfilling ways of balancing the imperatives of administration with faculty work. So far, albeit under great stress and sometimes neglect of my personal life, I have been able to remain fairly fresh and effective in my multiple roles, though, admittedly, there are low times.

Here is a sampling of my ongoing teaching: In fall 1998, as a voluntary commitment to teaching beyond my contractual obligations as dean of undergraduate studies, director of honors, and director of faculty development, I taught two sections of Honors 490M: The New Millennium: Past as Prologue" (20 students) and Orientation 190 (Honors): Freshman Orientation (21 students). The former was an interdisciplinary honors senior seminar instrumental in moving the institution forward in its mission of incorporating technology into the liberal arts curriculum; the course was linked to the NCHC Satellite Seminar, a live, web-based, interactive telecast. The latter is an academically focused freshman orientation, revealing my involvement in teaching students across all classifications, a commitment I have maintained as a dean and as a full professor to remain closely connected to all students. I also served as a first or second mentor to a number of honors senior projects.

In the last three years as dean, I have taught English 102 (H) twice to 15 and 18 students, respectively. I have, except for one semester since fall 1998, maintained a two-course load, a personal commitment to my students and my department above and beyond my contractual obligations as dean. In this same time period, I have advised nine majors and served as a special freshman academic advisor for 28 honors students across disciplines. (See my Teaching Portfolio in Appendix A for selective acknowledgements of my advising of both majors and honors freshmen on academic and personal issues, including email and other correspondences from students and alumnae whom I have advised.)

In addition to directing both honors and faculty development programs and serving as dean of undergraduate studies, I am the faculty representative to the athletics program for the National Association of Intercollegiate Athletics and serve on seven college and faculty committees, acting as chair of two, and on several ad hoc task forces (see Appendix C for list of faculty and administrative service activities and Appendix D for faculty and administrative service awards).

Philosophy of Faculty Engagement: Teaching, Scholarship, Service

Teaching. In my relations with students, I have learned that conscientious mentoring is a necessary dimension of transformative teaching and learning. Delivering information is a superficial act which the uninspired but competent teacher can perform. The outstanding professor knows the value of working patiently with students on personal levels. In a sense, the professor teaches more than content; he or she teaches habits of thinking, habits of being. Students discover in the process of engaged learning the rewards of controlled inquiry, the value of reasoned discourse, the delight of intellectual curiosity, and an earned respect for the process of questioning knowledge. Such values have directed my commitment to interdisciplinary collaborative projects with colleagues and students; samples are revealed in Appendices B and E.

Scholarship. The professor must demonstrate competency and currency by actively engaging in the public, professional venues of publications and presentations. The scholarship of teaching is an exciting dimension of change in higher education but should not replace the traditional arena of disciplinary research and publication, professional work that validates expertise among communities of scholars. Such charges fulfill the responsibility of faculty tenure and help a dean to be a credible administrative model for faculty (see Appendices E and F for samples of scholarship fostering a climate of faculty as well as administrative collaboration and reflective practice). I view such scholarly work as essential to my role as a dean whose chief calling is to inspire, support, and develop faculty and students.

Service. The dean and professor is also responsible for meeting the obligations of academic citizenship, for engaging meaningfully in institutional priorities and goals. My teaching portfolio documents how I have lived up to my own values and performance standards in teaching, scholarship, and service. This more comprehensive administrative/faculty portfolio adds another level of reflection to my professional growth, examining the interactions of my role as dean and my faculty identity.

Administrative Philosophy: Faculty Identity and Administration as Nexus

Reconciling the demands and responsibilities of administration with the related duties of the engaged teacher-scholar has been trying and exhausting. The challenges of my position as dean of undergraduate studies have pulled me necessarily in directions that have occasionally separated me from my vital work as a disciplinary teacher and scholar. Despite the tensions between my administrative and faculty roles and the difficulties of finding balance in my professional and personal lives, I have maintained a record of teaching excellence and high scholarly productivity in addition to the increasing, relentless responsibilities as dean. One positive sign of the interaction of my twin roles is that a fair amount of my scholarship recently has focused on issues of faculty development crucial to my work as dean of undergraduate studies. For example, I have been active as a consultant to several institutions nationwide on matters of teaching improvement and evaluation, curriculum review, program self-study, effective department leadership, and strategic planning (see Appendix E for list in Curriculum Vitae and Appendix G for sample consulting materials and evaluations).

Importantly, much of what I do as dean is developmental and supportive rather than evaluative. The particular details of my appointment as dean of undergraduate studies compel me to approach the position with a firm commitment to serve as a faculty and program advocate without the complications of traditional administrative authority. My position does not officially empower me to make decisions about hiring, tenure, promotion, program certification, or institutional funding.

Instead, I work with academic programs such as honors, faculty development, the Washington semester, contractual studies, the Collaborative Learning Center, women's studies, globalization and leadership initiatives, and the academic honor council, serving outright as the director of honors and faculty development. Consequently, I have consciously decided that if I can provide energy, inspiration, coherence, foundation, and support to individual faculty and to our strong, developing academic programs, then my philosophy of administrative leadership will have been realized.

My administrative effort, thus, has been to encourage and support various initiatives in undergraduate studies. I am still privileging my role and identity as a faculty member but learning to take more institutional perspectives on difficult issues and working harder to influence change, improvement, and community by example and by capitalizing on others' strengths while minimizing their or my own weaknesses. Such a philosophy of leadership stems from my convictions that an effective academic leader:

- Focuses on visionary, transformational goals.
- Inspires high expectations, academic integrity, and exemplary performance in others.
- Fosters a culture of collegial accomplishment, recognition, and reward.
- Values a strong ethic of collaboration, honesty, and fairness.
- Advocates for continual improvement and celebration of faculty and student achievement.
- Represents faculty and student voices and needs in institutional strategic planning and decision-making.
- Models the imperatives of engaged teaching, scholarship, and service by remaining integrally connected to faculty and students.
- Respects diversity, dynamism, and vitality of an academic community of learners.
- Manages responsibilities of administrative position effectively and ethically.

My philosophy has cost me, perhaps, a stronger presence on campus as a forceful administrator who issues powerful, unilateral directives, but my ongoing goal as an administrator and teacher-scholar is to make—as collaboratively and supportively as possible—substantive contributions to moving the college forward in its ambitious vision and strategic plan. I believe that such work is facilitated by administration, but it is the chief responsibility of faculty, working in concert to achieve the ultimate aim of enhanced student learning.

Hence, I conceive of myself as a fully engaged faculty member with additional administrative functions rather than the other way around. In several appendices, I include selective evidence of my continual care to communicate openly and clearly with my faculty colleagues, to be a resource for faculty and staff, to serve as a vital collaborator and mentor to others in the college community, and to share my own enthusiasm for and growing expertise in faculty development and other areas of administrative support in order to continue building the academic quality and reputation of the college. Appendix H, for example, contains a detailed description of my role as dean of undergraduate studies, a document I crafted to clarify and strengthen the work and influence of the dean's office on campus. Appendix I consists of brief descriptions of workshops on teaching portfolios, critical thinking, instructional technology, course assessment, department chairing, annual self-study, and other opportunities I have created at the college or in other professional venues to improve college teaching, learning, and administration. Appendix J documents encouraging electronic and paper communications with faculty, department chairs, and other administrators, announcing development opportunities or sharing resources; individual responses of appreciation are attached. Appendix K contains a record of my successful efforts as dean to revitalize and expand our recognition awards for faculty excellence; the appendix also includes evidence of my partnership with a friend of the college to memorialize a beloved faculty member by establishing the Savory Scholars Program, an endowed grants program for collaborative undergraduate research. Such work on behalf of faculty and student learning is the authentic charge of any academic leader.

Improvement and Evaluation of Performance as Administrator-Teacher

I have increasingly strengthened my effectiveness as an administrator-teacher by presenting at and attending numerous conferences focused on faculty development and academic leadership. For instance, I participate yearly in national meetings of the American Association for Higher Education, Professional and Organizational Development Network in Higher Education, Improving University Teaching and Learning, and Lilly Conferences on College and University Teaching, usually presenting sessions on fundamental issues in teaching, learning, or administration (see Appendix L for record of personal efforts to improve both administration and teaching and for further reflections on and documentation of how I have implemented development activities to strengthen performance).

One example of such targeted development is my collaboration with a faculty developer and a department chair from two other institutions to present on "Conquering the Scholarship Challenge: Encouragement and Evaluation of Faculty Scholarship" at the spring 2000 AAHE Conference on Faculty Roles and Rewards (see also Curriculum Vitae in Appendix E and accompanying documentation in Appendix F).

Another is a compendium in Appendix J of faculty listserv announcements, web postings, and other encouragements and sharing of resources intentionally designed to improve communication between me as a dean and faculty colleagues after an evaluation in 1999 by the provost indicated communication as an area for improvement (see Appendix M for all administrative evaluations and further documentation of strategies for addressing perceived weaknesses in my role as dean).

My work as a dean has not diminished my effectiveness as a teacher or scholar, as evidence in my teaching portfolio and record of publications and other scholarship will demonstrate (see Appendices A and E, respectively). But the demands of administration have occasionally cost me my department chair's perception that I have sacrificed some of the close, collegial relationships and quality time together that characterize our Department of English. In the teaching evaluation for the first year of my tenure as dean, my chair expressed some hesitation in delivering an outstanding rating because of the "small number of students that you teach" (the result of the half-time load I voluntarily teach) and the "number of times that you are out of town" (the result of many scholarly and administrative commitments). The assessment seemed gently disapproving of my unique balancing act as an administrator-teacher, but it prompted me to devote more time to departmental activities on top of my teaching, scholarship, and administrative responsibilities. I have improved my faculty evaluation considerably, earning a more appreciative appraisal from the department chair a year later: "John taught more than [his own] suggested load for his position, and during both semesters he interacted in the classroom with a larger number of students than might be expected because of the nature of his position as both administrator and professor. . . . I frequently consult him about problems . . . and despite his travels for his presentations, he is one of the first to respond to email requests and one of the most eager to discuss revision in our curriculum" (see Appendix M for evaluations and reflective analyses of improvement efforts based on specific feedback).

Improvement based on feedback from evaluations has been challenging, mainly because I am evaluated on two equal fronts: I submit completely to both administrative and faculty merit evaluation systems, a daunting task every year. But I am the one who insists upon the arrangement in order to preserve my full engagement as a faculty member while serving as an administrator. The dual evaluation, however, poses frustrating complications when improvement in one area creates tension in another.

My performance ratings in both administrative and faculty evaluations have been strong overall, though my faculty ratings are consistently exemplary, while my administrative evaluations are excellent but not uniformly outstanding. In 1999, for example, the provost's evaluation indicated perceived shortcomings in "mutual trust and understanding," the result of my passionate, intense advocacy of faculty and students in the midst of severe higher administrative problems and plummeting morale. My ratings in 2000 improved in the areas of administrative communication, partly because of my efforts but partly, perhaps more significantly, because of dramatic transitions that helped to defuse the tensions between faculty and higher administration, alleviating my own difficult position as a faculty-administrator (see Appendix M for record of improvement in administrative ratings). Still, having always prided myself on former presidents' and deans' superlative feedback on my performance as a teacher, scholar, and program director, I confess to slight dejection over small deductions in my two most current yearly staff reviews.

Nonetheless, I continue to thrive on exceptional, appreciative feedback from faculty and students, support that fuels my improvement as dean. For instance, in Appendix J, I document many qualitative comments from colleagues both within and outside my institution, revealing the extent to which I have dedicated considerable time and effort to make a positive impact on individual faculty, on the institution, and on the profession. A peer outside my department says, "I appreciate all you're trying to do to help us understand ourselves as part of the academy and to support each other as part of a special community." A colleague from another institution expresses thanks for my assistance in engaging faculty at his college and at other institutions nationwide in teaching improvement workshops: "Sincere thanks for the extraordinary mentoring you've done." Another professional colleague in the Council of Independent Colleges writes specifically to commend my contributions to the 1999

CIC National Institute: "John, several people went out of their way to let us know how helpful your session was.... Thank you for speaking at the CIC ... and we appreciate the work you did to help colleagues from throughout the country. Your session was highly rated." An administrative leader at another institution remarks about my work in faculty development, "John, I will always remember you because of the major contribution you have made to the scholarship of teaching." Doing the kind of faculty development work that generates such comments is one of the pleasures of administration.

A Dean's Work Is Never Done: Initiatives and Achievements
As dean this past year, I had a hand in too many initiatives to name individually—some routine, some unique—but perhaps among the most important and yet invisible were my extensive involvement in recruitment activities, my regular and personal support of student and faculty accomplishments, my efforts to strengthen college-wide progress toward academic excellence, and my commitment to helping actively with the valuable Washington Semester program. Selective evidence includes acknowledgements that I attended all the recruitment receptions and open houses on campus and out of town (see Appendix J for letters of thanks from admissions and for examples of email correspondences with prospective students) and numerous supportive communications with both faculty and students (see Appendix J for sample contacts with faculty and students across campus).

Another important dimension of administrative service to the institution is the support and confidence reflected in letters written for colleagues and students and in continuous written conversations with the campus community to maintain a high level of engagement in our academic culture. Appendix N includes selected letters written in the last three years, and Appendix J contains samples of animated discussions with colleagues about significant campus issues such as single-gender education, liberal arts education, and tenure and promotion. Such communications demonstrate my deep commitment to collaboration with faculty peers, a central dimension of effective administrative leadership.

For a catalog of major administrative accomplishments in a variety of areas that have fallen under my care as dean of undergraduate studies in the last three years, see Appendix O, where I list achievements such as:

• Increasing student caliber in honors

- Realizing 100% yearly retention in honors
- Expanding the Washington Semester from a half- to full-term experience
- Installing a women's studies program with a faculty director
- Successfully completing a self-study on globalization for institutional reaccreditation
- Revising and enhancing faculty recognition awards
- Inaugurating a collaborative undergraduate research program
- Multiplying opportunities for presentations of faculty scholarship
- Increasing faculty development funds by 62%
- Designing department development grants for collaborative scholarship and departmental renewal
- Restructuring the office of undergraduate studies to increase faculty ownership of academic programs

The appendix describes successful implementation of such initiatives, details my specific role in each, and adds reflective information about the valuable contribution of each to improving the institution's culture of academic excellence, the most important mission of administration.

Administrative Development Goals: Long Term and Short Term

1. My experience with teaching portfolios, peer collaboration, and faculty evaluation positions me as a strong advocate for reflective practice in improving teaching and learning. The college is embarking on crucial initiatives related to faculty performance, accountability, and rewards; I will be a key voice in strengthening institutional culture and making positive changes. I plan to recharge my continuing goal of staying involved in defining faculty roles and rewards on our campus by playing an active part in constructive reforms. Specifically, before fall term, I will offer a teaching portfolio workshop for new faculty to help incorporate them into a culture of reflective practice.

2. Next year, I will enhance the college's resources for faculty sabbaticals. Given the institution's strategic focus on earning national recognition as a liberal arts college, faculty scholarship will be key to moving ahead with a vision of strengthening our caliber and reputation.

Sabbatical resources need to be increased to encourage and support greater scholarly activity among faculty.

3. My administrative and teaching responsibilities compel me to continue distinguishing our students on the national level. Last year, I nominated students for Goldwater, Rotary, and Gates Millennium scholarships, helping one to earn selection at the local level for a Rotary and another to win a Gates. In my next year as dean of undergraduate studies, I will help our students compete for national awards such as the Truman, Marshal, Goldwater, and Rotary.

4. This summer, I will continue writing an invited book publication on learning portfolios. Such a volume will strengthen my work in the areas of teaching improvement and faculty development, enhancing my role as dean.

Appendices
A. Teaching Portfolio
B. Collaborative Scholarship
C. Faculty/Administrative Service
D. Faculty and Administrative Service Awards
E. Curriculum Vitae
F. Presentations, Publications to Improve College Teaching, Learning, and Administration
G. Consulting Materials
H. Role and Responsibilities of Dean of Undergraduate Studies
I. Workshops
J. Communications with Faculty, Students, and Administrators; Statements of Appreciation
K. Evidence of Support for Faculty Recognition and Faculty/Student Collaborative Research
L. Improvement as a Teacher-Administrator
M. Evaluations and Feedback
N. Letters Written for Colleagues and Students
O. Accomplishments as Dean

John Zubizarreta is Dean, Undergraduate Studies and Professor, English, Columbia College.

ADMINISTRATIVE PORTFOLIO
Joyce Hickson
Chair
Department of Counseling and Educational Leadership
Columbus State University
Columbus, Georgia
Spring 2001

Table of Contents

1. Introduction

The administrative portfolio: a personalized thumbprint. As a department chair at a mid-sized university, I view the administrative portfolio assessment process as a holistic means of monitoring progress and development over time throughout the duration of my administrative assignment. It is important to me to gather instances of development, growth, and markings that indicate significant developmental leaps and aspects of professional maturity. The portfolio also provides a means for reflection and the opportunity to critique my work in a meaningful way while serving as a measure of evaluating the effectiveness of interactions with the various constituencies served.

The institutional context. Columbus State University (CSU) is a public comprehensive university serving approximately 5,500 students. There are four colleges: Arts and Letters, Business, Education, Science, and the Schwob School of Music. Additionally, there is a graduate council and a program of continuing education. The university serves the educational needs of a diverse region by providing a mixture of liberal arts and professional programs leading to associate, baccalaureate, and graduate degrees. The institution places a major emphasis on teaching although it also recognizes the role of research and service.

The departmental context. The present Department of Counseling and Educational Leadership experienced a number of transformations. In 1991, counseling as an academic discipline was first established at CSU. At the time of its establishment, this discipline was merged with the existing disciplines of special education and reading, and I was named chair of the newly reconfigured department. The new department, renamed The Department of Counseling and Clinical Services, added two graduate degree programs, Community Counseling and School Counseling. In 1998 another reorganization took place, and counseling was housed with the graduate programs of Educational Leadership. This remains the official designation. The intervening years since 1991 have evidenced the growth in enrollment of the two counseling graduate degree programs, school and community counseling, from the initial number of 12 majors to the current figure of 125 majors. Moreover, there has been the addition of an EdS program in School Counseling, and the addition of three counseling specialty tracks: pastoral counseling, student personnel counseling, and marriage and family counseling. The discipline of Educational Leadership also experienced growth after its merger with the discipline of counseling. Along with MEd and

EdS programs, a doctoral program in Educational Leadership was added in August 2000, representing the first doctoral program at CSU. With its two disciplines, the department currently serves over 300 students.

2. Department Chair Responsibilities

At CSU, the departmental administrator responsibilities are defined as 1/3 administration and 2/3 teaching, research, and service. In truth, I spend the greatest percentage of my time on administration. Personnel resources are as follows:

- 12 full-time permanent faculty

- 15 part-time faculty

- 3 graduate assistants

- 3 work study students

- 1 administrative secretary

At various times I serve as a teacher, mentor, researcher, leader, planner, manager, mediator, evaluator, supervisor, coordinator, recruiter, decision-maker, problem solver, and peer-colleague. My role also necessitates that I facilitate departmental governance with respect to conducting department meetings, the establishment of department committees, and the preparation for accreditation and evaluation, as well as developing long-range department programs, plans, and goals. Another role I have is that of recruiting and selecting faculty members and assigning their responsibilities in the areas of teaching, research, and service. Additionally, I serve as academic leader in regard to instruction, curriculum, and scheduling and also oversee faculty performance and development. Moreover, I oversee student recruitment and retention and the advising of current students. Communicating with both internal and external constituencies is a job responsibility as well as managing budget and resources. Office management of clerical and support staff is part of my portfolio as well as the maintenance of essential department records and the monitoring of department security and equipment. A special and very important role is that of anticipating and bringing about change in a time of economic uncertainty, changing enrollment, new technological delivery systems, and new factors influencing student priorities. In my role as a department chair, intervention plans, leadership, decision-making, and creating a vision for the future are integral parts of the equation. And so is the art of survival.

3. I Wanted to Be a Chair: Now How Do I Cope with the Stress?
When I took the position of department chair in 1991, I honestly believed I would be selected into the administrators' hall of fame. A piece of cake, I thought. Little did I know that I would soon be trotting out Selye's classic book, *Stress Without Distress,* and digging out my yellow legal pad notes on Wolpe's relaxation techniques. Burns's *Feeling Good* also became part of my growing library. Every time I heard television commentators point out the association between stress and illness, my ears perked up, and I indeed asked myself on more than one occasion, "How did I get into this job?" Keeping a daily journal helped immensely as a tool of ventilation and a means for identifying common sources of stress. Some of my stressors were as follows:

- Playing tug-of-war between the faculty and the administration and feeling caught in the middle between opposing demands

- Dealing with the isolation of being one of the group and yet not really being a part of the group due to my assigned position as leader

- Responding to edicts from higher authorities and external constituencies and having to be the messenger in explaining these demands for innumerable and meaningless reports to faculty

- Mediating conflicts between students and faculty as well as personality conflicts between faculty, and dealing with staff concerns

- Dealing with difficult colleagues

- Responding to legal challenges from irate students who did not get accepted into a competitive counseling program

- Keeping calm in the midst of demands upon my time such as constant interruptions, innumerable meetings, and ringing telephones

- Conducting the periodic evaluations of job performance of faculty and staff and dealing with colleagues who view the procedure as threatening

- Learning to deal with the frequency, intensity, and duration of stress

I have learned to deal more effectively with the stress by realizing that I've been trying too hard to be perfect. I've also identified my greatest stressor as that of dealing with difficult, combative people. Accordingly, in my professional development plan I make sure that I attend two or three workshops each year dealing with this topic, and I review my material from these sessions on a weekly basis. Amazingly, this technique really has helped. I now sally forth into battle non-defensively and spend a great deal of my time listening non-judgmentally. I genuinely try to understand where the other person is coming from, and I try to be on an equal plane as we move into collaborative problem solving. Another coping strategy that has been effective is that of engaging difficult colleagues in casual conversations that are not work related and periodically visiting them in their offices. In these encounters, I am able to exercise my humanity, thereby appearing less intimidating and more approachable. I am cognizant of the fact that I still need to gain more expertise in the area of intervention strategies. Conflict resolution and the use of conflict in a productive manner remain as professional goals of self-improvement.

4. Philosophy of Best Practice

My philosophy of leadership has evolved from a high-directive approach to that of a low-directive, negotiative approach. I believe the maturity level of the group must be acknowledged and that newly formed groups often need direction and support in order to function efficiently and in order to achieve specific goals and objectives. The newly established Department of Counseling and Clinical Programs in 1991 represented a conglomeration of faculty who had not worked with one another as a unit and in a collective way. Many of these faculty were also new to academe. In keeping with situational dynamics, a directive approach was appropriate. Currently the department exhibits the maturity of seasoned academics who have the experience, capacity, and willingness to work effectively as a group, set high but attainable goals, and reach group decisions. Accordingly, I now spend less time being directive and more time being supportive.

As a leader I try to continuously learn and to help the faculty and staff in my department learn. We can learn from one another. For example, a faculty member with expertise in clinical supervision is conducting in-service training for the counseling faculty in this area. Another faculty member has shared his expertise in technology. I believe that faculty have different gifts to give one another and that the strongest department is the one that makes use of faculty resources. I believe one gift I have is that of conducting research, and I have partnered with almost every faculty member in the department in the production of journal articles.

Collaboration is a major value, both in research activities as well as presentation activities.

I believe I do a particularly good job in gathering information and resources that can be used in shared decision-making. As the designated chair, I also believe it is important to try to be able to see many perspectives, not just my own. There is strength in diversity of opinion. An emphasis is also placed on creating a vision for the department, having a sense of mission, and setting and reaching goals and objectives. These activities are important in order to give the department a sense of movement and progress.

A major approach to leadership is that of trying to get the department to function as a team. I want to be a leader with a small "l." I strongly believe that leaders who emphasize teamwork and team effort are more valuable than leaders with a big "L." It is very important that faculty be stakeholders and that collaboration, mutual support, and involvement are built. For example, on occasion at department meetings I ask various faculty to lead the meeting. Additionally, at department retreats I ask additional faculty to lead the department in goal setting and strategic planning. These activities represent professional development activities for individual faculty members and contribute to making the department stronger. Finally, a key question I ask myself is, How do I want to be perceived as an administrator?

My Administrative Tombstone
I started out as an administrator in 1991 wanting my colleagues to think of me as super intelligent and as a prolific writer. I now want them to think of me certainly as being competent, but more importantly as being kind and concerned about their welfare. This is what I hope they experience and what I hope my legacy will be.

5. Performance Evaluation
  Personal performance

- Letter from Columbus State University's president inviting participation in Executive College, November 30, 2000: "Selection for participation in the Executive College Program is truly an honor and also recognition of an individual's potential and capacity for advancement within our university." (Appendix A)

- Letter from dean, College of Education (Annual Performance Review, April 2000): "Dr. Hickson continues to provide strong leadership to the Department of Counseling and Educational Leadership." (Appendix B)

- Letter from associate dean of the College of Education, April 2000:

- "Dr. Hickson is a conscientious professional who takes her job seriously and can be counted on to go above and beyond what is required in her job." (Appendix C)

- Letter from director of grants and sponsored programs, February 2001:

- "Professor Hickson, as a department chair, has made invaluable contributions to the administrative academic aspects of CSU. She is a valuable asset to our institution." (Appendix D)

- Letter from director of judicial affairs, February 2001: "Dr. Hickson is an outstanding department chair. Her many accomplishments speak for themselves. I commend her." (Appendix E)

- Letter from member of a College of Education standing committee, Intellectual Vitality and Learning Climate Committee, November 2000: "I find Dr. Hickson to provide a supportive, collaborative style of leadership and to create an environment within the committee that promotes synergy and creative achievement." (Appendix F)

- Letters from graduates of the Community Counseling program, September 2000 and February 2001: "As my teacher, Dr. Hickson gave me the necessary room to grow by showing faith and confidence in my ability. She treated me with respect and more as an equal than a student." "Your presentations were always exceptional and I was honored to be supervised by you. You're a great mentor." (Appendix G)

Program performance

1. The survey of graduating counseling students (2000), with a return rate of 70%, indicated that 90% of graduates believed they were well prepared in their training program, and 10% believed they were adequately prepared.

2. The survey of current students (2000), with a return rate of 95%, indicated a positive view of the program while giving constructive comments for improvement. Student orientation was viewed positively as was receiving helpful feedback on assignments. A high rating was also

received on the quality of advising, and students were grateful for the opportunity to do cooperative research projects with their professors. The fundamental tone of respondents toward aspects of teaching and program activities reflected a positive attitude with representative individual comments as follow:

- "Great experience—continue to improve."

- "Great program! I have grown professionally and personally, and I am actually a better person for having gone through the program."

- "My overall experience in the program has been positive."

3. Practitioners and graduates reviewed the CSU Educational Leadership programs August, 2000. Results included the following positive comments:

- "Program standards should be kept high."

- "Retain the amount of time spent on student interaction and teamwork."

- "Courses place the field of study in proper perspective."

- "Course content was related to current school problems."

- "Instruction was related to students' needs."

- "Courses interrelate."

- "Field-based components were valuable."

- "Course instructors have experience," "professors have practical knowledge," "professors gave individual attention."

Constructive comments were made about the need for flexibility of scheduling and an improvement in technological delivery systems.

6. Professional Development Activities

In order to address the issue of learning to deal with conflict more effectively and learning to be a better communicator I have attended the following seminars:

Seminars and workshops

- How to deal with chronically impossible people (January 2001)—8-hour workshop, Skill Path Seminars, Columbus, Georgia. This workshop taught me how to deliver constructive feedback and how to choose the most appropriate intervention techniques when dealing with employees with negative behavior patterns.

- How to be a great communicator (June 2000)—8-hour workshop, Fred Pryor Seminars, Columbus, Georgia. I learned to assess my own communication effectiveness and strategies for dealing with difficult interpersonal situations.

- Communication skills for administrators (May 2000)—8-hour workshop, Dr. Lin Inlow, Georgia Board of Regents, Columbus, Georgia. This workshop taught me how to deal with difficult people and difficult situations.

- Negotiating skills for administrators (April 2000)—8-hour workshop, Dr. Lin Inlow, Georgia Board of Regents, Columbus, Georgia. I learned bargaining and positioning skills and how to understand the other person's agenda.

Currently, I am participating in Executive College, a CSU program designed to prepare managers, administrators, and supervisors to utilize theories, principles, and practices of organizational behavior. Each module is covered in five 8-hour days. The modules covered this year are as follows:

- Leadership and team building, January 2001, office of the president, Columbus State University

- Human resource management

- Fiscal management

- Legal issues and trends in public agencies

- Strategic policy and development for the 21st century

- Management and decision-making

Thus far, I have attended one module, leadership and team building, which covered how to create workplace communities through the principles of coordinating, collaborating, and creating. Additionally, I learned to assess my own style of leadership and how to employ flexible leadership styles in the context of different situations.

Technology

- Grant proposal funded November 2000 in the amount of $3,500 by the Georgia Institute of Technology (Georgia Tech) to receive training in advanced and intense technological programming.

- Grant proposal funded 1997–1999 in the amount of $5,000 by the University of Georgia for distance learning education.

Books

The following books have been read during the past year:

- *Who Moved My Cheese?* (S. Johnson, 2000)

- *Enhancing Departmental Leadership* (J. Bennett & D. Figuli, 1993)

- *Chairing the Academic Department* (A. Tucker, 1993)

7. Significant Administrative Accomplishments

- Secured $50,000 in Georgia educational grants to work with low performing schools and to improve teacher quality (2001).

- Implemented two new graduate counseling programs, Community Counseling and School Counseling, one new EdS program in School Counseling, and three specialty counseling track programs (Pastoral Counseling, Student Personnel Counseling, Marriage and Family Counseling) at CSU (1991–present).

- Served as academic leader in securing CSU's first doctoral program, the EdD in Educational Leadership (August, 2000–present).

- Established collaborative partnerships between CSU and universities in South Africa (University of the Witwatersrand, 1991–present) and China (Shaanxi Normal University, 2000).

- Academic leader in successful self-studies and accreditation visits by the Council for the Accreditation of Counseling and Related Educational Programs (CACREP) and the National Council for the Accreditation of Teacher Education (NCATE).

8. Institutional Improvement

- In securing the Council for the Accrediting of Counseling and Related Education Programs (CACREP) accreditation for the counseling programs, the department became one of only three schools in

Georgia to successfully attain this. accreditation, joined by the University of Georgia and Georgia State University.

- The department was awarded a contract from the U.S. Army to train its chaplains in marriage and family therapy and to train them for leadership positions within the Army.

- Results of Praxis, an Educational Testing Service (ETS) graduate test outcome, indicate pass rates of 94% and 95% for School Counseling and Educational Leadership students, respectively.

- The department has produced the first web-based journal in the field of counseling, *The Journal of Technology in Counseling*.

- The listserv for the field of counseling, Counselor Education and Supervision Network (CESNET), is operated from the department.

- The first doctorate for the institution is the doctorate in Educational Leadership, administered by the department.

- As part of the educational reform movement, the department was awarded a grant to assess and improve low performing schools and a Title II teacher quality grant.

- The chair of the department was the only professional in the College of Education to be selected by the institution's president for Executive College, an advanced leadership training opportunity.

- Faculty in the department established and published the first journal for the College of Education, *Perspectives in Learning*.

9. Organized Programs

As department chair, I organized the following events and programs:

- Dean's Award for Innovation, 1998–present

- First annual College of Education Fall Celebration, November 2000

- Scholarship awards to Muscogee County Teachers, May 2000–present

- Sponsorship of College of Education's first visiting professor: Professor Xiaoduan Chen, Vice-Dean of Faculty, Shaanxi Teacher's University, Xi'an Province, China, Fall semester, 2000

- Delegation leader for mental health and educational delegation to South Africa, 1997, 1998; Delegation leader for mental health and educational delegation to China, 1999

10. Administrative Awards

- College of Education's Research Award nominee for CSU Honors Day, April 2001. This nomination was made by the COE administrative council in recognition of my research and grant activities.

- College of Education's Service Recognition Award, spring banquet, April 2000. This award was presented by the dean of the College of Education for instructional initiatives in implementing CSU's first doctoral program, the EdD in Educational Leadership.

- American Counseling Association's award, Contributions to International Education, 1999. This award was presented by the chair of the ACA International Education Committee as recognition of my involvement in establishing collaborative partnerships with mental health professionals in South Africa and China and for establishing links with international educational institutions.

- Association for Spiritual, Ethical, and Religious Values in Counseling (ASERVIC) Research Award, 2000. This award was presented by the ASERVIC organization for my research in the area of the inclusion of spirituality in counseling older clients.

11. Professional Development Plan

My profile would indicate that I am a well-organized planner who is systematic and consistent, goal directed and time focused. I use facts, figures, and information for intelligent decision-making. I am open to other ideas. I believe that I need to grow in the area of creative thinking and that I also need to be aware that at times I advance my own agenda rather than using the kind of collaboration that is needed. Along this same vein, because I am so goal focused I need to pay more attention to group process and less attention to task accomplishment.

I also would like to further improve my administrative skills, and my participation in Executive College will help me work on this goal. I particularly want to learn more about human resource management and management and decision-making.

Another area I would like to achieve a greater expertise in is that of technology. I have already attended approximately ten 8-hour sessions in email, word processing, PowerPoint, etc. However, I would like to have a greater understanding of how to develop Web CT courses.

I would like to continue to develop my skills in the area of communication and constructive conflict resolution. I intend to continue attending workshops in these areas.

Future administrative goals
My major administrative goal is that of mobility in the organizational setting within the next three years. I aspire to be director of graduate education for the College of Education. Graduate education is presently a part of my portfolio, and plans are to develop an Office of Graduate Education.

12. Appendices

A. Letter from Columbus State University's president inviting participation in Executive College

B. Letter from Dean, College of Education

C. Letter from Associate Dean, College of Education

D. Letter from Director of Grants and Sponsored Programs

E. Letter from Director of Judicial Affairs

F. Letter from Member of Intellectual Vitality and Learning Climate Committee

G. Letters from Graduates of Community Counseling program

Dr. Joyce Hickson is Chair, Department of Counseling and Educational Leadership, Columbus State University.

ADMINISTRATIVE PORTFOLIO
Cathryn Amdahl
Writing Program Coordinator
Harrisburg Area Community College
Harrisburg, Pennsylvania
April 2001

Table of Contents
1. Introduction
2. Primary Duties
3. Administrative Philosophy
4. Administrative Objectives and Methods
5. Workshops/Services/Programs I've Provided
6. Five Most Significant Accomplishments
7. Evaluations from Supervisor and Colleagues
8. Goals for Next Five Years
9. Appendices
    A. CASS Guide to the Evaluation of Part-time Faculty
    B. Targeted Teaching Strategies Handout
    C. Designing Writing Assignments and Analyzing Student Writing Workshop Evaluation Results
    D. Handouts: "Building Common Ground: Integrating Multicultural Diversity in the Writing Class"
    E. List of Workshops
    F. Annual Evaluations from Supervisor
    G. Evaluations from Colleagues
    H. Proposal for Improving Part-time Faculty's Working Conditions

Introduction

Purpose. I intend this portfolio to document my philosophy, responsibilities, and effectiveness as writing program coordinator at my community college. I've created it primarily to help others evaluate my work and make necessary personnel decisions, but I also intend for the portfolio to assist my efforts at improving both myself and the writing program.

Description of my institution. Harrisburg Area Community College (HACC) is a public, two-year commuter college in central Pennsylvania. About 12,000 full- and part-time students are enrolled in Associate of Arts or diploma programs. The Wildwood campus in Harrisburg, where

I work, serves the largest number of students (about 10,000), while two other campuses and a center serve others regionally. About 200 tenure-track teachers and about 700 part-time teachers work at the school.

Description of the writing program. Students in all transfer degree programs and most diploma programs are required to complete two writing classes. About 17 tenure-track writing teachers and about 50 part-time writing teachers instruct these classes, which include basic writing, freshmen composition I and II, technical writing, and business writing. Ours is an open-admissions school, and about 15% of students are placed in basic writing for their first writing course, while others enter freshmen composition based on the effectiveness of a short entrance essay they write.

The writing program has no budget of its own. As writing program coordinator, I report to the dean of the Communication, Arts, and Social Science Division.

Neither a writing-across-the-disciplines nor a computer-assisted writing program exists, though elements of such programs are in place. Most students are given the chance to write short answers to questions on exams and research papers in various disciplines, and most faculty across the school have had some training in the teaching of writing. For the past three years, we have offered one section each of three different writing courses (composition, business writing, and technical writing) online.

Primary Duties of the Writing Program Coordinator
This coordinatorship is a part-time position of 22.5 hours per week during the academic year and full-time in the summer. The coordinator's primary duties and the approximate percent of time devoted to each include:

- Staffing about 45 sections each semester of adjunct-taught writing classes (10%)

- Hiring, orienting, and mentoring an average of five new part-time teachers each semester (20%)

- Supervising the writing course placement essay procedure for about 1,500 students each semester (20%)

- Reviewing the syllabi, assignments, grading practices, and student evaluations for about 35 part-time writing teachers and mentoring these teachers based on those reviews (30%)

- Helping the part-time writing teachers at the branch campuses as needed (10%)

- Helping community members and other disciplinary teachers with writing projects (10%)

During the academic year, the coordinator teaches six credits of writing classes and is expected to fulfill the committee work and academic advising expectations of all tenure-track teachers. This means the coordinator teaches about 50 students, advises about 20, and spends about five hours each week on committee work.

Administrative Philosophy

At our school, as at many others, a substantial number (about 56%) of the required writing courses are taught by part-time teachers. My administrative philosophy recognizes that part-time teachers don't receive benefits or equal pay for equal work. (At our school they receive $2,100 for teaching as many as 26 students in a 15-week writing class.) Part-time faculty are not paid to attend professional development programs. Perhaps the most important principle I follow is this: Don't further exploit the part-time faculty. I also follow these other guiding principles in my administrative work:

- We are all in this together. The more minds, the merrier. Knowledge is a social construction.

- My most important job is supporting a community in which everyone is welcome, and everyone is needed. I am here to find out what people need and to help them get it.

- Schools should be meaningful and fun places.

- We are all more than a sum of our faults.

- There are many ways to get to heaven. Teachers' individual approaches to teaching should be supported.

- We should question authority.

- Writing programs should be grounded in best practice research.

Administrative Objectives and Methods

The writing program coordinator's most important task is to hire, orient, evaluate, and mentor adjunct writing teachers. My primary objective for this job is to provide an integrated approach that is fair to the adjunct teachers and helps them develop professionally, while ensuring that students receive writing instruction based on the best practices nationally. Toward that goal, I focus my attention on recruiting and hiring part-time teachers who 1) understand the conditions of their part-time status, 2) want to use their experience at our school to develop professionally, and 3) have a sense of humor and the demonstrated ability to work well with a variety of students.

I think the most important help I give new teachers is to assist them in writing their syllabi, which are key components in their evaluations and professional development. Writing the syllabus requires teachers to articulate their philosophy, the course goals, their strategies for achieving the goals, their plan for the entire semester, and the ways they will evaluate students' work. In reviewing the syllabus, I can help teachers prevent problems and ensure that they are in line with course goals and school policies.

The dean of my division and I developed an evaluation system that describes how the syllabus is best developed and how we evaluate teachers based on their syllabus (see Appendix A).

The other important instrument I use to integrate hiring, orientation, evaluation, and professional development is the Student Evaluation of Educational Quality(SEEQ) program. At the hiring stage, I find out the strategies the teachers use in the areas of teaching effectiveness measured by the SEEQ. In orienting and mentoring them, I keep focused on those areas by giving them some of the best practices gleaned from teachers who are rated highly in the areas by students (see Appendix B). I also review samples of their assignments and comments on student's papers with the SEEQ areas in mind.

I help teachers use the SEEQ results from their students by asking them to target the less highly rated areas (one at a time) and then plan one or two specific teaching techniques to improve that rating the following semester. Evaluation, thus, is always formative. At the hiring stage, I make clear to part-time teachers that they will be asked to continue teaching if their syllabus is complete and thoughtful, if they meet deadlines, and if the SEEQ results after two or three semesters are adequate.

Workshops/Services/Programs I've Provided

- About 15 workshops on various aspects of the hiring, evaluating, and mentoring of part-time teachers, including two at the National

Adjunct Guild Conference ("Hiring and Evaluation of Adjunct Faculty," 4 January 1997, Washington, DC and 3 April 1998, Chicago).

- Workshops and consultation with about ten adjunct teachers each semester from disciplines other than writing about designing writing assignments and responding to student writing (see Appendix C for workshop evaluation results).

- About 15 workshops on integrating issues of pluralism and diversity into writing classes (see Appendix D for handouts).

- Workshops on various topics for all faculty including "Teaching Strategies to Increase Students' Learning," 4 January 2001; "Using the SEEQ to Improve Classroom Instruction," 5 January 2000. (See Appendix E for a complete list of workshops I've offered since 1992.)

Five Most Significant Accomplishments During the Coordinator's Term

- Improved syllabi from part-time faculty. Because grading practices, teaching philosophy, and course calendars are now explicit in syllabi, fewer students complain about their teachers to the dean or to me.

- Improved part-time faculty evaluation. Clear expectations and a standardized student evaluation instrument (the SEEQ) are now in place.

- Improved writing course placement practice. Students are no longer placed in writing courses based on a computerized test of their sentence-level skills. Rather, students are now placed based on the quality of essays they write.

- Multicultural diversity issues are now integrated in all writing courses.

- Improved practices for hiring and orienting adjunct writing teachers. Teachers are no longer hired at the last minute and receive individual orientation to the school and the writing program.

Evaluations from the Coordinator's Supervisor and Colleagues

Supervisor evaluations. Below are excerpts from annual evaluations from my supervisor, Mike Dockery, Dean of the Communications, Arts and Social Science Division (see Appendix F for the complete evaluations).

"Adjunct writing teachers are now producing far clearer, more detailed syllabi because of Ms. Amdahl's work." (Annual review 1996–7)

"Ms. Amdahl's work with writing course placement readers and her work on the new placement practice are good illustrations of her excellent initiative and ability to work with others." (Annual review 1995–6)

"Cathryn Amdahl continues to contribute significantly to the division and to the college with her excellent work on improving working conditions for adjunct teachers, her work on improving syllabi, and her work on writing course placement practices." (Annual review 1999–2000)

Colleague evaluation. Excerpts from evaluations from my colleagues are below (see Appendix G for complete evaluations).

"Cathryn's participation in college activities has been exemplary. Over the years, her activities have included the CA& Placement Exam Committee, The Task Force on Instruction, The Wildwood Writer's Conference, The Writing-to-Learn Task Force, and the HACC Heritage Festival." (Peer review committee's recommendation for tenure report, September 1996)

"Cathryn, you were so much fun to work with. You helped me more than you can ever know." (Bernadette Ernakovich, former part-time writing teacher, December 1999)

Goals for the Next Five Years

- Propose a college-wide integrated model for hiring, orientation, evaluation, and professional development of all adjunct faculty. Proposal to be submitted to faculty council by January 2002.

- Implement a computer-assisted writing program. Upgraded computer lab installed by January 2002 (dependent on successful Title III grant). Training of teachers completed by March 2002. Twenty-five computer-assisted writing classes offered in Fall 2002. All composition courses to have online syllabi, chat rooms, and web links by Spring 2003.

- Assess the developmental writing course and plan improvements. Assessment completed Winter 2004. Improvement proposal submitted by Spring 2005.

- Help improve the employment conditions: salary, benefits, professional development support, and status of part-time teachers. (See Appendix H for proposal.)

- Work to ensure that all core courses build students' writing abilities. One workshop on assigning and evaluating student writing each semester for the next five years.

Appendices

A. CASS Guide to the Evaluation of Part-time Faculty

B. Targeted Teaching Strategies Handout

C. Designing Writing Assignments and Analyzing Student Writing Workshop Evaluation Results

D. Handouts: "Building Common Ground: Integrating Multicultural Diversity in the Writing Class"

E. List of Workshops

F. Annual Evaluations from Supervisor

G. Evaluations from Colleagues

H. Proposal for Improving Part-time Faculty's Working Conditions

Cathryn Amdahl is Writing Program Coordinator, Harrisburg Area Community College.

ADMINISTRATIVE PORTFOLIO
Jane S. Halonen
Director
School of Psychology
James Madison University
March 2001

Table of Contents

Introduction

Purpose. The purpose of this portfolio is to document my current administrative responsibilities and my effectiveness in my role as director of a school of psychology at a comprehensive university. I have assembled the portfolio to clarify my current responsibilities during a time of reorganization and change on our campus, contribute creatively to discussions about new possibilities, and facilitate adaptation to my changing role as well.

Institutional context. James Madison University (JMU) is a public comprehensive university with a nationally recognized reputation for quality with nearly 15,000 enrolled students. JMU has made a dramatic transition from its origins as a normal school for women, specializing in the training of teachers, to a coed institution with a justified reputation for innovative general education, coherent specialization in majors, and niche programs in graduate education. Five disciplinary colleges organize 47 major fields of undergraduate study. The inauguration of a new president, his appointed Centennial Commission, and a newly appointed vice president of academic affairs coalesced to challenge constituents of the campus to think about the possibility of innovative administrative structures to support new ways of interdisciplinary collaboration.

The School of Psychology. The School of Psychology provides undergraduate and graduate education in psychology as well as an on-campus clinic for training students at both levels. The undergraduate program attracts between 800 and 850 majors, making it the largest undergraduate major at JMU. The school houses seven graduate programs, including five masters/educational specialist degree programs and two innovative doctoral programs with an applied focus.

Administrative Responsibilities on Campus

School of Psychology. The responsibilities related to the director's position include the following:

- Direct supervision and evaluation of 44 psychology teachers and 4 secretaries, including recruitment, retention, career advising, and opportunity facilitation

- Support and leadership for academic programs and their coordinators

- Management of Executive Council (program coordinators, an untenured faculty representative, and our executive secretary)

- Supervision of $3.4 million budget and oversight of additional grant funds

- Allocation of resources across programs

- Advocacy of high standards for quality teaching, research, and service

- Promotion of psychology's activities and interest to the campus at large, the community, and relevant professional organizations

- Representation on various campus task forces and planning groups

- Communication and conflict resolution
- Advocacy for faculty resource needs and grant development
- Oversight of maintenance and improvement of physical plant in two academic buildings

JMU campus

- Co-coordination of ongoing new faculty orientation program
- Co-coordination of unit heads meetings
- Co-chair of Eastern Teaching of Psychology Conference
- Chair of Faculty Inauguration Committee
- Member, Diversity Initiatives Team

Statement of Administrative Philosophy

I believe that the best administrators combine several crucial characteristics, including being egalitarian, fair-minded, trustworthy, straightforward, and accessible. They should be advocates for the groups they serve, but they should also be responsible for gentle developmental assistance. Administrators should collaborate appropriately to promote group cohesion and effective decision-making; sharing as much information as possible and minimizing secrets facilitates this outcome. However, they also should distinguish when faster action may be required and be able to withstand the backlash if such decisions prove unpopular. Administrators should empower and trust those whom they supervise to avoid the complications and disarray of micro-management, but they have the obligation to pay attention, offer feedback regularly, and assist supervisees to understand their collective actions in the larger context. I believe the most successful administrators own and apologize for their mistakes and then facilitate moving on to the next challenge. They foster charitable responses to inevitable human error. I also believe that academic administrators should be active scholars and should render service to the groups that serve departmental interests and their personal values. Given these lofty ideals, it helps if administrators have a creative flair for managing resources, money, and time. They should place high value on facilitating the best quality of life related to work as possible.

Administrative Strategies

Weekly newsletter. I communicate regularly with faculty, graduate students, and important adjuncts once a week by emailing *Notes from*

School, a compendium of reminders, news, and announcements that cuts down on email traffic and advertises our activities. (See Appendix A.) I publish the newsletter faithfully every Wednesday. The *Notes* are also published on the web at <cep.jmu.edu/psycalendar>. I receive regular positive feedback about the newsletter's helpfulness, timeliness, and humor. Some graduate students even refer to me as Notes.

Topic-focused school meetings. Once per month I meet with the faculty and staff on topics that allow us to address large issues of interest to the School of Psychology (ethics, collaborative opportunities, faculty evaluation strategies) since the newsletter takes care of more routine business and announcements.

Email as religion. I spend significant time answering and generating email on behalf of the department. I rarely allow the queue to get long. I also use email to consult with colleagues in similar positions throughout the country. Although I am not entirely happy with the degree to which email has become a dominant mode of working, I strive to maximize real human contact wherever and whenever possible.

Open door practice/office visits. My door is literally open most of the day onto the busiest corridor in our building. I encourage faculty, staff, and students to drop in for informal visits. I also make a point to stop in to see faculty in their offices. This practice connects me to faculty and encourages an opportunity for deeper conversation than email.

Administrative collaboration. I meet weekly with the directors of the undergraduate and graduate programs. I convene the Executive Committee biweekly and offer opportunities for that group to shape the discussion agenda. In addition, I meet biweekly with the College Steering Committee. The college dean and I discuss the school's progress in monthly meetings.

Activities Undertaken to Improve Performance

Systematic assessment. The College of Education and Psychology conducts an annual evaluation that assesses performance by category (exceptional, professional, needs attention, no basis to judge) in the spring semester to assist with the annual performance review. I conduct a formative assessment at the close of the fall semester. I ask the faculty to respond to selected dimensions of performance or give them the option of writing a summary that will help me shape my activities on their behalf. Qualitative commentary from this survey will be excerpted in a later section. A copy of the most recent summary of their ratings is in Appendix B.

Exit interview feedback. We conduct a comprehensive assessment of graduating seniors and specifically question them about the quality of interactions they experienced with the director. The last round of results indicated no areas for improvement.

Involvement in training workshops. I participated in an American Council in Education Seminar for chairs as part of an administrative team sent by JMU. As a result of that activity, I helped to activate a regular meeting for unit heads to discuss common concerns and innovative solutions to problems. The group meets on a monthly basis.

Regular reading. I read the *Chronicle of Higher Education, Change,* and *AAHE Bulletin* regularly. I often transmit articles of specific interest to faculty and use the content of the articles to assist in strategic plans.

Innovations and Effectiveness Assessment

I have been in my position as director for a little over 2.5 years, following a particularly beloved administrator. The generosity and endorsement of the former director helped me to continue the tradition of a strong positive work climate. Enthusiastic faculty and staff cooperation with the transition facilitated the following achievements.

Revision of the annual review process. Our faculty had evolved into the practice of producing monster portfolios that presented their materials less selectively, making it difficult for our elected Personnel Advisory Committee (PAC) to review and make performance judgments efficiently. The PAC and I streamlined the process, adding a reflective component and a formal self-assessment for merit determination. The more efficient process has been popularly received, and we continue to refine the process annually.

Improved diversity climate. JMU has received negative feedback broadly in program reviews for its lack of progress in promoting diversity, a difficult challenge in rural academic settings. I re-instituted a departmental Diversity Committee within the school. We established an alliance with the Psychology Department of Howard University that resulted in recruiting a Howard ABD to teach full-time for us. We organized a reception for undergraduate majors, which is becoming an annual tradition. We dedicated a school meeting to discussing practical strategies for diversity recruitment and retention. We also collaborated at the campus level to have a reception for minority community leaders and faculty members. The Diversity Committee is currently crafting a mentoring program for our minority undergraduates.

Expanded public recognition. I work conscientiously with our JMU public relations representative to maximize publicity for the school. I actively pursue honors on behalf of the faculty that will bring appropriate attention to their accomplishments. This advocacy was a contributing factor to the faculty in the school receiving one regional and four national awards in the past few years, with a few more in process. In turn, this achievement produced greater on-campus coverage. (See Appendix C.) I also have added a tribute component to upcoming and recent retirements to highlight the career achievements. We display the faculty portraits with tributes written by their colleagues in the lobby of our main building. We also will be expanding recognition of good performance with the first honors reception for faculty and students in the spring.

Improved work environment. Shortly after arriving at JMU, I convened a meeting with the president, academic vice-president, and dean of the college to review the insufficient and dilapidated space available to the School of Psychology. I prepared a humorous videotape that illustrated our needs in a non-threatening manner. Within the year, we gained sufficient space in a building close to our primary site that accommodated our research needs and created better meeting space. Since we had no budget, I recruited donations from local merchants to furnish some of the spaces. I initiated other aesthetic improvements throughout our two primary buildings.

Ongoing attention to quality of life concerns. Our campus is teaching-intensive, which has resulted in a 12-unit standard load with substantial service and research expectations. With the endorsement of our academic vice-president, I am working with our program directors and coordinators to develop more tailored and streamlined assignment of responsibilities. These plans will reduce the teaching obligation to nine hours for those who are productive with their research programs or student teams or those who are teaching primarily graduate courses. Changes have been implemented in many of our programs with no decline in morale.

I consider the professional support staff to be critical to the success of our mission. I include them in all communications, encourage flexible work hours, convene systems meetings to help solve collective problems, and promote the ability to work as collaboratively as possible as a way of facilitating working from their individual strengths.

Participation in Other Activities Related to Academic Administration

I take great pride in the work that I have contributed to the Society for the Teaching of Psychology. I am the past-president and serve on the Long Term Planning Committee. During my presidential year, I chose the theme of crossing boundaries to promote an expanded vision of the way this group could serve teachers of psychology. I currently chair a task force on developing strategies for the preparation of future psychology faculty, which involves promoting an alliance across multiple groups interested in faculty development.

I serve as an advisor to many groups interested in the promotion of improved teaching. These include serving as an advisory board member to Improving University Teaching, which sponsors an international teaching conference each summer. I am a member of the planning committees for the following national conferences: the summer National Institute for Teaching of Psychology (July 2001), Project Kaleidoscope (July 2001), and the 1st National Conference on Psychology Assessment (September 2002). I also serve as an advisor to Educational Testing Services' (ETS) New Constructs Project to redefine the SAT and *Discovering Psychology*, the long-running PBS television series on introductory psychology, hosted by Phillip Zimbardo, which is being revised and updated.

Ludy Benjamin of Texas A&M University helped me discover the world of high school psychology teacher development with his invitations to serve as an invited faculty member at his summer NSF-funded workshops. I have nurtured this interest with involvement in the development and reading of the Advanced Placement Test in Psychology. I am scheduled to become the chief reader for psychology in 2004. I have been a featured speaker at nearly every high school institute in the country. I have also served as the faculty advisor in the development of the National Standards for High School Psychology and for the Teachers of Psychology in Secondary Schools, sponsored by the American Psychological Association.

I have donated significant service to the American Psychological Association. I have served on multiple planning groups and task forces, including Preparing Future Faculty in Psychology, Task Force on Psychology Outcomes, the Psychology Partnerships Project, and the St. Mary's Conference on Improving Undergraduate Education in Psychology.

Faculty development concerns drive my consulting activities. I have completed over a dozen department reviews, specializing in assisting departments that have gotten bogged down in contentious relationships. I have served as a consultant to general faculty, conducting workshops or presentations in the following areas: ethics, civility, faculty-student boundaries, critical thinking, writing enhancement, assessment, and impact of technology on faculty performance.

Self-Evaluation

One of my favorite Gary Larson cartoons shows a party scene with a group of bored looking sheep. One of them has opened the door to show a rather crazed-looking dog. "Everything's going to be all right," says one of the sheep. "The border collie's here." Although this metaphor should not be pressed too far, there is a lot of the tail-wagging, intense, eager-to-work border collie in my administrative style.

I was fortunate to have inherited some proclivity for management from my parents. My father worked as a manager at a custom sports car factory in Indiana. He helped me develop a love for solving problems and to understand that managers must contend with the unexpected. My mother was an executive secretary with strong organizational and social skills, which I strive to emulate.

My evaluation data suggest that I have been very successful in achieving most of my departmental and personal objectives. I have been disciplined about completing the multiple tasks of my job, for the most part accurately and punctually, although I continue to struggle to find the right organizing schemes that will reduce some absent-mindedness. Faculty and staff describe my communication style as straightforward and accessible. Nearly all of the faculty report feeling satisfied with my administration, despite the challenges of having significantly fewer resources than we need compounded by operating during a period when the organizational landscape may be changing.

I enjoy collaborating to promote shared interest and mission, but I do not shy away from making difficult and sometimes unpopular decisions. I strive to be as accessible as possible and to listen actively and nondefensively. I am grateful for a strong favorable evaluation bias that allows me to frame others' actions as positively as possible until proven otherwise. I have rarely been disappointed when striving to see the best in others.

Although I'm blessed with an unusual amount of energy, I try not to invest that energy in micro-management. I trust the program coordinators and support staff with whom I work and strive to find ways to make their jobs easier.

However, the formal and informal feedback I've received suggest I need to be more conscientious about some aspects of my style. I can sometimes be impulsive, acting on what I think is a good idea before I have invested sufficient time and energy to bring the rest of the group along or to pursue feedback that would improve the idea. Occasionally my sense of humor strikes a sharper note than I intend. Although it is mostly successful, I've also learned that my own direct style sometimes creates obstacles where a softer style would be more effective.

Tensions can develop quickly in times of limited resources or when the future feels ambiguous. We have had both conditions this year. I need to remember the natural tendency for faculty to be more protective of the programs in which they have invested so much rather than expecting them to give priority to the needs of the school as a whole. I need to learn more about the specifics of the programs in the school. I have sometimes misread the politics that influence decisions outside of the school and have been trying to be more vigilant regarding potential opportunities as well as inevitable challenges.

Although I am effective in managing multiple tasks and meeting deadlines, I wonder about whether I am working efficiently. If I could figure out better methods for managing time, I would invest the time saved in expanding our funding from resources outside of the State of Virginia. I rarely achieve a sense of closure on the work involved in my role, and although I prefer the crisper markers inherent in teaching life, I have learned to adjust.

Administrative Recognition
The American Psychological Foundation honored me with its Distinguished Teaching Award in 2000, in part for my administrative support of high quality teaching and my contributions to curriculum development in psychology. (See Appendix D for citation.)

Testimonials Regarding Performance
Appendix E provides a series of testimonials regarding my contributions. The appendix is divided into descriptions of performance related to campus concerns as well as feedback related to administrative leadership in off-campus activities.

Administrative Goals: Short Term and Long Term
Short-term goals

- Facilitate faculty ownership of changes in function and structure that lie ahead.

- Develop strategies to enhance more effective collaboration across programs.
- Promote improved quality of life by evaluating resource and time investment.
- Use my humor more judiciously to avoid creating unintentional offenses.
- Negotiate a renewable term of service for my position.
- Collaborate on design of honors reception that is celebratory, yet noncompetitive.
- Improve impulse control on email communications.
- Master efficient operation of my Palm Pilot.

Long-term goals

- Contribute creatively and proactively to evolution in institutional reconfiguration.
- Improve my knowledge of program requirements and working conditions.
- Expand external sources of funding.
- Maintain scholarly productivity.
- Evaluate my fitness for leadership in the emerging administrative structure.

Appendices

A. *Notes from School* (Weekly newsletter to faculty, staff, and students)

B. Summary of Quantitative Feedback on December 2000, Formative Evaluation

C. "JMUniverse" Article on the School of Psychology

D. Citation for Distinguished Teaching from the American Psychological Foundation

E. Selected Testimonials

Jane S. Halonen is Director, School of Psychology, James Madison University.

ADMINISTRATIVE PORTFOLIO

Monica A. Devanas
Director of Faculty Development and Assessment Programs
Teaching Excellence Center
Rutgers University
New Brunswick, New Jersey
February 2001

Table of Contents

Introduction—Description of Rutgers University

"Rutgers University is the flagship institution of New Jersey's public higher education system. It is a vibrant and diverse community of 49,000 students and more than 10,000 faculty and staff. The university comprises 29 undergraduate colleges and graduate and professional schools, as well as over 130 specialized research institutes. Some 175 academic departments offer 270 bachelor's, master's, doctoral, and professional degree programs. Dedicated to a three-fold mission, Rutgers is equally committed to excellence in teaching, scholarship, and public service. And driving all of Rutgers' activities is the defining characteristic of a premier research university: the continuous and vigorous creation of intellectual capital—the new discoveries and insight that drive advancement of human knowledge and contribute to the improvement of the human condition." (Rutgers. *The State University Fact Book, 2000–2001).*

Purpose of the Administrative Portfolio

The purpose of this portfolio is to review my duties and my effectiveness as (formerly) associate director and now director of faculty development and assessment programs of the New Brunswick Teaching Excellence Center at Rutgers University.

Description of the Teaching Excellence Center

Rutgers University is fiercely proud of its research reputation. As a member of the American Association of Universities since 1989, there are many incentives for scholarly excellence. But even with the considerable focus on research, faculty members are committed and concerned about undergraduate education and effective teaching. The notion of a Teaching Excellence Center (TEC) was an idea initiated by faculty, incubated for almost a decade, and finally funded in 1991. Each campus of Rutgers (Camden, Newark, and New Brunswick) has a TEC supporting campus-based functions. However, the New Brunswick TEC is additionally responsible for the newly initiated university-wide Student Instructional Rating Survey process. Unique among teaching centers, the New Brunswick TEC has both assessment and development responsibilities.

The global mission of the New Brunswick Teaching Excellence Center is to promote the enhancement of teaching. Toward this end, the center offers services in faculty development, evaluation, assessment, and support for projects using instructional technologies. The New Brunswick TEC is also responsible for the university-wide Student Instructional Rating Survey process. Some of the data from this summative assessment are used in the teaching statements for reappointment and tenure, as well as for merit pay allocations. As director of faculty development and assessment programs, it is my responsibility to oversee this process, guarantee the integrity of the data, distribute the data to the libraries, and maintain the official archives.

With the Student Instructional Rating Survey in place, and an office for support and development, the request of the faculty to be rewarded for good teaching was given some framework. The reappointment and tenure process was changed to include comprehensive descriptions of teaching including significant data points derived from the Student Instructional Rating survey data: Rate the instructor compared to the department, and rate the course section compared to all other courses offered in the department. Now these data are also being used for merit pay allocations. Like an overnight success in the theater, our hard work and scrupulous methods have generated what seems like a sudden adoption, if not enthusiastic interest in these quantitative data. Also included in promotion and tenure materials are questions about faculty development initiatives, workshops attended, curricular innovations, and evidence of the scholarship of teaching.

Starting the Teaching Excellence Center was very much like starting a dot-com in one's basement. The spirit of entrepreneurship was found in all aspects of the center, from unloading cases of forms from trucks, to creating canapés for receptions, to writing our own program, and taking the entire survey process in house, we did it all. The founding staff of the TEC were the director, Gary Gigliotti, economics professor and technically half-time; Georgean Jolly, administrative assistant; and myself, the full-time members of the team. Despite our small numbers, many programs emerged, and some continue to have long lasting and wide impact on the entire university.

Administrative Responsibilities

I began my career in faculty development with the beginning of the Teaching Excellence Center. My only teaching credential was a recently won Faculty of Arts and Sciences Dean's Award for Outstanding Contributions to Undergraduate Education. However, I had been teaching for 20 years as a graduate student, in microbiology courses, laboratories, prep rooms, to nurses and medical students, to poets and philosophers. Even as a graduate student, my advisor acknowledged my innate teaching talent. To me, teaching was something one simply did, but whatever the venue, I did it well. I am thrilled to explain complex biological phenomena to scientifically naïve students and see their eyes widen in understanding. Now I marvel at finding years of research authenticating the strategies and methods that I thought I invented. I find my passion in teaching extends now to my colleagues as I explain active learning or critical thinking and see them nod in understanding. After 20 years working as a microbiologist, the responsibilities of the associate director and then director of faculty development and assessment programs of the Teaching Excellence Center were, and continue to be, both challenges and opportunities.

Key duties

1. Direct and manage distribution and processing of the university-wide Student Rating Survey. Among the associated responsibilities are the design and development of special versions of the Student Instructional Rating Forms. I design specific forms for special teaching situations such as the Citizenship and Service Education program, Cooperative Extension programs, and Continuing Education programs. In addition, I also design and direct the preparation of special reports on the Student Instructional Rating System data for vice-presidents, provosts, deans, and department chairs.

2. Design, organize, and present faculty development workshops, seminars, programs, and consultations on teaching, curriculum, and assessment through the Teaching Excellence Center. There is special emphasis on workshops in the development and use of instructional technologies, all of which I have used in my own teaching. I have also coordinated all the activities of the various TEC teaching fellows programs: the Lilly Endowment Inc. Teaching Fellows, the RU Teaching Fellows, and the General Electric Learning Excellence Fellows.

3. Consult with deans, chairs, and faculty members on the development and construction of teaching portfolios, methods of peer review, and all other activities involved in the creation of robust evaluation of teaching for merit consideration, promotion, post-tenure review, and general self-development of faculty expertise in teaching.

4. Seek external support for TEC activities, implement and assess grant-funded programs for faculty development and instructional technology.

5. Represent the Teaching Excellence Center on the Faculty Council Committee on Teaching Effectiveness, the Faculty Library Committee, the Academic Coordinating Council, the Rutgers College Residence Life Academic Advising Committee, and the University College Academic Affairs Committee.

Reflective Statement

The principles that have infused all of my activities of the Teaching Excellence Center are:

- To be above reproach in all dealings with faculty and faculty matters, but especially with respect to the data generated by the Student Instructional Ratings

- To be responsive to the individual needs of all members of the university community, particularly faculty members in development initiatives

- To recognize that newly hired faculty have vastly different needs than mid-career faculty; faculty in professional schools versus liberal arts; adjuncts, graduate students, agricultural extension specialists— all have unique and special needs

- To anticipate new directions in trends of higher education and find ways to appropriately manage the changes

In establishing any faulty development initiative, the most critical element underlying all activities must be trust. This is particularly the case for the TEC since it was given responsibilities for both assessment and development. The faculty must trust that survey data are valid, reliable, and secure. The faculty must trust that counseling sessions are completely confidential. Without trust, no meaningful relationships can exist. In all the activities of the Teaching Excellence Center, every effort has been made to be principled in our support of faculty. The center was conceived and implemented by faculty and continues to serve the faculty's best interests in all its functions.

The TEC has worked hard to earn the trust of both the faculty and the administration. The highest complement in this regard came when both the faculty and the administration called on the TEC to provide data on teaching effectiveness. Clearly we have become the trusted archive for these data.

Faculty development is a broad structure under which many initiatives can be housed. I believe that support for faculty can mean anything from consulting on a frustrating classroom situation, to coaching someone through the development of online courses, to designing and evaluating new degree programs. All of these needs are part of faculty development. To address them, I offer workshops, visit departments, make presentations to graduate student groups, videotape faculty in the classroom, and practice both the traditional classroom visitation as well as provide an online version for anonymous formative student feedback (http://TeachX.rutgers.edu "TEC Services" "Mid-course online survey").

The interests of faculty in teaching extended beyond their day-to-day interactions with students in lecture halls. As more and more faculty reflected on their student feedback, they began to ask questions about how to teach better. They also asked for more comprehensive assessment strategies such as the teaching portfolio. Once the process of assessment and evaluation of teaching became part of the culture, the next need was for structures for peer review. All of these interests were addressed by the TEC.

As far as my duties to oversee the Student Instructional Rating Survey, I believe that every faculty member, every instructor, every staff support person involved in the process should understand both the process and the value of the results. Every interaction is important. Additionally, I believe everyone should understand the extent to which the results are used, could be used, and are useful both for formative and summative issues. Toward that end, we have run focus groups, made presentations, testified before committees, explained to deans and chairpersons, and have created a very comprehensive web site to provide information (http://TeachX.rutgers.edu see Appendix A). Still, I am happy to handle calls from faculty needing to understand the manner in which a mean is determined, whether comparisons are made with other departments, or requests to send the departmental collection of data for the last five years because the disks and files cannot be located.

The students also have many needs, both for information about their education and the plethora of computer-based tools that have been used to develop and enhance their courses. The TEC has been responsible for regular interactions with students to explain the purpose, relevance, limitations, and outcomes of their ratings survey. Meetings with student groups, infomercials in visited classes, even articles in the student newspapers (see Appendix B) have been used as vehicles to inform the students. To assist students with the instructional technology tools, we have created tutorials online on our TEC website and run workshops for the more elaborate software packages for students in courses using these tools (see http://TeachX.rutgers.edu).

Technology has been a significant lever to move some faculty to consider their teaching and course design. I believe that teaching can be enhanced with the use of the array of course tools that are available. I have worked hard to be an exemplar of these methodologies. No matter how long a faculty member has been teaching or how ensconced in style he or she might be, the use of Internet resources and computer-assisted teaching are vehicles to address pedagogy. These technologies can be useful if and only if better pedagogy is the focus and the software is the tool. I have used each of the various technologies as they have been developed, so that in turn I can speak validly about their useful applications. One can no longer walk into a classroom and talk. Students today at Rutgers expect web pages for each course, descriptions of assignments, and the number of papers and exams. Part of my job is to help faculty with these transitions and in the process improve their teaching too (see Appendix C for list of workshops).

Five Most Significant Accomplishments

Student Instructional Rating Survey. First and foremost among the successes of the TEC is the creation, development, implementation, and refinement of the Student Instructional Rating Survey process. Prior to the implementation of the university-wide survey, few departments had formal reviews of teaching. We have worked long and hard to produce a system that is trusted, respected, and appreciated by the faculty. If we did nothing else, this one accomplishment was worth the struggle.

Fellows/faculty development. Financial support for faculty development from outside the university has been another important accomplishment. Such support indicates that the quality of the supported programs is exceptionally high and seen as vital for higher education.

- **1997–2001:** To assist the development and implementation of good pedagogy through the application of instructional technologies tools to courses in the College of Management. This grant, funded by the General Electric Foundation, specifically addresses the challenges of merging business departments across two campuses, the blending of faculty and students, and most significantly, using state-of-the-art business tools in the learning activities of the students

- **2000–2001:** As co-principal investigator on a New England Resource Center for Higher Education (NERCHE) grant funded by the Kellogg Foundation, my responsibilities are to assess the expansion of the Citizenship and Service Education programs and to assist in the design and implementation of a certificate program in service learning for graduate students.

Curriculum design. Four new courses are now being offered for non-science majors. These courses were the outcome of a National Science Foundation Institution-wide Reform of Science Education grant. The grant proposal used my "Biomedical Issues of HIV/AIDS" as a model for science education for non-science majors. The success of this course (the most popular single-sectioned course, with a class size of 450) is due to the extensive use of active learning, critical thinking, inquiry/discovery teaching and learning strategies, all in a large lecture format. I was happy to assist with the proposal, implementation, and assessment of these new courses in life sciences, chemistry, physics, and mathematics.

- **1998–2000:** To design, develop, and implement effective methods of integrating research methodology into teaching. I have been co-principal investigator on the National Science Foundation Institution-wide Reform of Science Education grant. I arrange for significant workshops, seminars, and lectures by national experts in science education to inform NSF Senior Science Fellows and the faculty at large about the state-of-the-art methods that can be used in their own parts of the project, their new courses. I have also worked with the director of the Math and Science Learning Center to plan, organize, and deliver research workshops for undergraduates interested in developing research expertise in the sciences.

Master Practitioner of Instructional Technology
Prior to my assuming this position at the TEC, my concept of instructional technology was the use of colored chalk. Since then, I have used every technical tool possible to first train myself and then to train others in the usefulness of such tools as email, listservs, web pages, streaming video, and course packages with bulletin boards and chat rooms. If there is a way to improve teaching with or without technology, I will learn it, practice it, and then teach it to others.

The Student Instructional Rating Survey Process

The implementation of a student rating process, although supported by many faculty and the Faculty Council, was not unanimously welcomed. Just as with students who may not have studied sufficiently, assessment feels like a threat, and some of the faculty were reluctant to consider student feedback on the classroom learning environment. So, when I started as the associate director of the Teaching Excellence Center, I had clear direction on that matter: "Keep your head down, and keep the place running." My director wisely decided to field the political mortar while I did what I do best—develop faculty. Since that time, I have basically launched a new career in faculty development. I have attacked the field in a manner similar to my science training: Read all you can, go to workshops and meetings, seek consultation with experts, learn at every opportunity, and teach what you have learned to others.

The early years of the Teaching Excellence Center were marked by great success of the Student Instructional Rating Survey. Within three years, we had significantly shifted the environment from one of fearful apprehension of student assessment to acknowledgement that the process had merit, was valid and reliable, and even was useful. The first task was to redesign the survey instrument, which had been designed by committee. The current form was redesigned during the first year of TEC operations with as much faculty input as possible. The form is designed to ask formative development questions (see Appendix D) and two summative questions that are used in personnel decisions. The analysis provided also has undergone revision with both faculty and administrative input and approval. Ultimately the Faculty Council, the advisory faculty body for the campus, voted to publish the results of the Student Instructional Rating Survey by having them on reserve in the library. Now the challenge is to move the data into a web-based access format, since many faculty and students are requesting Internet access to the information.

As the survey process for student feedback became increasingly more useful for departmental organizational management, some departments saw their unique needs for specialized feedback and requested that additional questions be added. In some cases, the data are customized for departmental needs. For example, the astronomy and physics department believes that style of teaching is critical and has the data for their department analyzed in five categories: introductory lectures, advanced lectures, recitation, workshop, and laboratory.

Evaluation Data

As with most small businesses, rarely did we have time to think about the program we just did before it was time to run the next one. Hence there are few forms of quantitative data that we can point to to support our claims to success. Instead there are many qualitative measures. Perhaps the ultimate in success measures is the bottom line. During the past eight years, each of the founding staff have been promoted: Gary Gigliotti to full professor, Georgean Jolly to administrative assistant, and me, as my position was redefined from associate director to director of faculty development and assessment programs. Additionally, the TEC gained two more full-time staff lines: Marcia Anszperger, as director of staff training programs, expanded the TEC; and Joseph Delaney, originally instructional technology specialist, was promoted to associate director. Budget increases for the staff training and Student Instructional Rating Survey have also been made by the central administration (see Appendix E for TEC Annual Report).

In regard to the survey, faculty experts in assessment repeatedly examined the Student Instructional Rating Survey for its validity, reliability, and authenticity. Their reports were shared with the faculty and the university community. The limited analysis that we have done on the Student Instructional Rating Survey process indicates that the data from Rutgers courses are consistent with national reports and decades worth of research. The same trends in student satisfaction are seen in our data: The humanities typically rate better than the social sciences, which in turn rate better than the sciences. We monitor these data as we compile reports for deans.

The evaluation of workshops offered by the TEC is clearly evidenced in the consistent praise from the faculty and staff alike. Susan G. Forman, Vice President for Undergraduate Education, and Professor Kathleen Scott, President of the University Senate, have offered letters of support. Faculty members report the great value that the workshops have for them (see Appendix F). Whether it was a workshop on instructional technology, curriculum design, or teaching portfolios, I try my best to be an expert practitioner.

Rutgers University has had in place for many years a very rigorous performance appraisal system for administrators and staff. Each spring supervisors submit informal reports to staff, followed by formal appraisal review. During my time at the TEC, I have received superior evaluations, merit awards, and a promotion. The Rutgers University Administrator/

Professional/Staff Performance Appraisal for me for this past academic year 1999-2000 can be found in Appendix G.

Professional Recognition

To demonstrate my expertise in these areas, I offer the information that I have been invited to speak about instructional technology in a variety of faculty venues, including presenting the keynote at the Michigan State University, College of Human Ecology Faculty Day (see Appendix H for list of presentations). The American Association of Colleges and Universities has nationally recognized my work in curriculum design. My course, Biomedical Issues of HIV/AIDS, has been nationally recognized as a Science Education For New Civic Engagements and Responsibilities course (see Appendix I for letter of award). The unique curriculum design model that I developed with this AIDS course has also been described by Jean MacGregor in her recent text on learning communities, *Strategies for Energizing Large Classes: From Small Groups to Learning Communities* (Jossey-Bass, 2000). The model is to host the AIDS course as a life science general education offering but link to it independent study seminars in various departments which are taught by faculty who have AIDS research interests; i.e., HIV in journalism and mass media, HIV and public policy, women's studies, psychology, human ecology, and education, among others. As far as acknowledgment of my expertise as a mentor for faculty in preparing teaching portfolios, I have been invited to join the team of Peter Seldin (Pace University). He is the international expert on teaching portfolios, and I am very honored to be included on his team as he consults with faculty around the country.

Evidence of Impact

The criticism that the student survey was not sufficient for the evaluation of teaching was an initial complaint of the faculty. The answer to this was the implementation and now widespread use of teaching portfolios. Formalized peer review processes, initially present in only a few departments, have been growing in interest and application. The (Rutgers University) Cook College faculty have voted as a faculty body to require teaching portfolios in all personnel decisions, following several series of workshops and consulting periods on the process. Likewise, the Cook College Teaching Effectiveness Committee have asked for my consultation and now are working on a peer review process.

The evidence of impact of the TEC and my role in it can be measured by the steady growth of our programs both in variety and support. We have found that many faculty appreciate the meetings and workshops at the TEC where they can network across departments and schools. Others find that workshops developed specifically for departmental concerns are more relevant; i.e., teaching portfolios, peer review, or accreditation preparation. Now many request online resources where they find outlines and suggestions to use and come for follow-up development meetings. Other indicators of success are the attitudes of the faculty, chairs, deans, provosts, vice presidents, and even the president. If there are any questions about teaching issues, teaching effectiveness, evaluation, and assessment of teaching, the TEC is called.

Over the past eight years, the TEC as been fortunate to have funding for faculty development initiatives that have brought instructional technology tools to many faculty members. The faculty were first supported with TEC funds through a series of small grants to faculty for teaching initiatives. Larger grants then funded departmental proposals. In both models, faculty were rewarded for initiatives, but some faculty fellows have gone on to transform their own schools and departments to be leaders and models for computer-assisted teaching and learning. (See Appendix J for lists of TEC grants and Lilly Fellows, RU Teaching Fellows, and General Electric Learning Excellence Fellows, National Science Foundation Senior Science Fellows.)

In our pursuit of improving teaching, the issue of classroom environment has been addressed in a variety of ways. The TEC has been asked to assist in the design of smart classrooms complete with audio and visual equipment, computer connections for projection, and connections to the Internet. The introduction of instructional technology tools and the coordination of delivery of technology require the cooperation of many different offices at Rutgers. Early on it became apparent that offices such as computing services, the library, media services, television and radio production, key early adoptors among the faculty, and key individuals from deans' offices needed to communicate and coordinate our efforts. This consortium of technology delivery offices has been successful in gaining entry into an elite group of institutions and corporations, the New Media Center (http://www.newmediacenters.com). Through the efforts of this committee, many significant technological innovations have been successful, including the funding for a faculty development computer laboratory at the TEC.

The mission of the TEC extends beyond faculty, staff, and students, even the university community. Frequently we are hosts to visitors from around the world with issues and questions about higher education, instructional technology, and faculty development. Some of our recent visitors have been officials from Oman, Moldova, Georgia, and Kazakhstan: the director of the Center for Human Resources and Staff Development, Sultanate of Oman, Sultan Qaboos University; the rector of Moldova State University along with a Member of Parliament and the chief of the Cathedra of Industrial Chemistry; from Georgia, the rector of Shosta Rustaveli Batumi State University and the vice rector of Gori State University; from Kazakhstan the vice rector of academic affairs and international relations, Al Farabi Kazakh National State University; and the rector of East Kazakhstan Technical University. The state department has graciously sent letters of thanks for the successful visits of these leaders in higher education, and I was presented with the Moldova State University medal (see Appendix K).

Efforts to Improve Performance

Efforts to improve both the various programs at the TEC and my personal skills have been numerous. I frequently attend national and international meetings, taking part in relevant workshops. I have been a member of The Professional and Organizational Development Network (POD) and attended their annual meetings since 1994. The pre-conference workshop for new faculty developers, Getting Started in Faculty Development, was particularly useful. Many other topics have been very critical to my development: using student ratings of instruction, problem-based learning, critical thinking, learning styles, and building a comprehensive faculty evaluation system. From learning styles to group testing, I have returned to campus with new strategies, new methods, and new energy to present, implement, and distribute these ideas. Many insights into the unique issues of the TEC and Rutgers can be obtained by having experts and authorities visit campus. When these experts come to campus, they contribute presentations or workshops to the faculty, and I get to absorb their expertise and build programs for the Rutgers-specific needs. Among the notables invited to the TEC have been Peter Seldin, Barbara Millis, Karl Smith, Lion Gardiner, Robert Diamond, Brenda Laurel, Barbara Duch, and Steve Gilbert.

Goals

In responding to the ever-demanding needs of our university and faculty, I have several goals in mind for the next three years. I would like to develop an evaluation and assessment center at the TEC. This center would provide scanning services for exams and surveys. In addition to the scanning, the TEC would assist the faculty in curriculum design with integrated, meaningful assessment and evaluation.

Faculty development is typically conceived around a traditional teaching faculty; i.e. teaching in classrooms within specific courses. Through my consulting with faculty at other institutions and across Rutgers, it is evident that new structures are evolving that will require faculty development, such as online courses and programs. In these structures, pedagogical considerations are most critical because virtually the entire course needs to be created before encountering students. Most times the technical infrastructure is unstable, and alternate delivery methods and materials need to be prepared.

Personally, I would like to expand my faculty development skills to include instructional and programmatic design. Rutgers University is constantly inventing and reinventing programs, departments, and even schools. I would like to be able to assist more effectively in the creation and successful implementation of these new initiatives.

Appendices

A. The Teaching Excellence Center Home Page

B. Sample Student Instructional Rating Survey form, *Targum* Student Newspaper articles, December 2000

C. Workshops for Faculty

D. Sample Promotion and Reappointment Teaching Effectiveness Spreadsheet

E. Teaching Excellence Center Annual Report AY 1999-2000

F. Letters from Faculty:
    a. Susan G. Forman, Vice-President for Undergraduate Education
    b. Kathleen Scott, President, University Senate
    c. Professors Shannon Martin and Shalonda Kelly

G. Performance Appraisal Review, 1999-2000

H. List of Presentations

I. Letter of Award from the American Association of Colleges and Universities

J. Lists of Fellows

K. List of International Visitors, Letter from State Department

Monica A. Devanas is Director, Faculty Development and Assessment Programs, Rutgers University Teaching Excellence Center.

ADMINISTRATIVE PORTFOLIO
Christina DePaul
Director
Myers School of Art
The University of Akron
January 2001

Table of Contents

1. Introduction

Purpose. The purpose of this document is to gather information and to document my effectiveness as the director of the Myers School of Art. It is intended to identify my strengths and improve my weaknesses.

Mission of the Myers School of Art. It is the mission of the Mary Schiller Myers School of Art of the University of Akron to provide a quality undergraduate education in the visual arts within the context of an open admission university. The Myers School of Art combines a strong foundation program with high quality programs in eight studio areas as well as art history and art education. The faculty consists of practicing artists, designers, and scholars who combine a dedication to excellence in teaching with creative and scholarly practice. The large number of faculty offer a diversity of approaches to art. An excellent faculty-to-student ratio and faculty mentoring allow extensive individual instruction.

We offer two degrees designed to meet the needs of both our traditional and nontraditional students. The BA emphasis affords an opportunity for those interested in a broad background in the arts or work in related fields, while the BFA provides solid training and preparation for professional practice and lifelong learning. We recognize that there are many kinds of excellence. Our mission is to define and encourage these within our diverse student body.

It is also our mission to offer our expertise and resources as professionals to the Akron and northeastern Ohio community. Strong exhibition programs, visiting artists, and lecture series that are open to the public are one way to accomplish this. We also encourage our faculty to provide leadership and services to the community as working artists, designers, speakers, exhibition jurors, and consultants.

2. Statement of Administrative Responsibilities

I am the chief administrator and supervisor of the Myers School of Art, which is accredited by the National Association of Schools of Art and Design. The school consists of 27 full-time faculty, 25 to 30 adjunct faculty, 3 contract professionals, 6 staff members, 500 art majors, and 840 students taking art classes. I oversee a 65,000-square-foot building with 12 studio/labs, 5 computer labs, a visiting artist studio, 2 galleries, a slide library, and an auditorium.

I recommend changes in curricula and appoint faculty members to various positions and/or committees. In conference with the dean, I make recommendations on reappointments, non-reappointments, promotions, tenure, salaries of the faculty and staff, and new appointments of faculty. Another responsibility is making sure that we meet the National Association of Schools of Art and Design standards and overseeing all strategic planning for the school. I work closely with faculty to develop their goals and to celebrate their accomplishments.

To a great degree, I am involved in development for the school. I work very closely with potential donors and have been largely responsible for increasing the school's endowment from $25,000 to $6,000,000.

I have established a school advisory committee made up of community members and alumni and also serve on committees and boards in the community.

Recruitment and retention efforts are an additional area of responsibility. I host events for high school art teachers and interested students as well as for students enrolled in the program. The Student Advisory Committee to the Director keeps me informed of students' concerns. In addition, I:

- Manage a budget of $2,282,000 and further endowments over $6,000,000.

- Am responsible for enforcing policies and systems within the school.

- Serve on university committees and am actively involved in the campus fine art and design committee.

- Am an advocate for the faculty and serve as the reporting link between the faculty and the dean.

3. Statement of Administrative Philosophy and Methodology

I am very comfortable with people and find it easy to talk to anyone. I lead by the heart and the mind and try to be in touch with my faculty on an emotional level while simultaneously engaging their intellectual level. Being a leader of so many innovative and creative individuals is a privilege and a challenge. I love knowing what they are thinking and why. The challenge is how to incorporate these ideas into the mission of the school. I encourage much discussion, probably at times too much! But by doing so, I can better understand the complexities and perceptions of many thoughts. As a result, I am more informed about the people that I am working with: their strengths, beliefs, desires, weaknesses. This knowledge helps me to strengthen the school.

I consider any issues that can change someone's life a priority over anything. Personal issues, issues of conflict, lack of motivation, all can impede a school's progress. I resolve these issues immediately by getting all parties involved, if appropriate, in a discussion. The dialog does not end until a resolution is agreed upon by everyone involved.

Constantly trying to take the school to the next level of excellence, I keep creative energy flowing. By doing so, I need to be acutely aware of how the faculty and students are thinking and what keeps them motivated. I believe in autonomy within the School of Art, but need to be informed of all that is going on for the smooth running of this large unit.

Working on a daily basis with the assistant director to assess projects and deadlines and other related areas is imperative. I have staff meetings weekly to discuss events taking place and work with a planning committee consisting of representatives from each area of the school. We meet bi-weekly to discuss new ideas to implement, problems to correct, and future planning of the school. I invite faculty to the discussion if it pertains to their area or if they are interested in the particular topic of discussion. A smaller number of faculty for discussion works better for the flow of ideas. The information discussed is then presented to all faculty at the regular faculty meetings.

Heavily involved in faculty development, I raised an endowment to ensure that funds will be available to the faculty for their creative research. I meet with each faculty member to discuss their goals, work on a plan to help them achieve these goals, and encourage them to apply for funds both within and outside the school. By doing these things, I am involved with their goals and thus can better understand their particular interests of research and their working styles. This helps me to think of ways to fund their research, identify their strengths, and incorporate those strengths in the school. It also gives me a wonderful opportunity to celebrate their successes.

I participate actively in fundraising activities and spend many hours with potential donors extolling the quality of our school. In addition, I work very closely with the college development officer thinking of new ideas and creative ways of funding them. We work very well as a team and have brought many new opportunities to the school.

I work personally with every level that makes up the culture of my school, from the president of the university to the students. Part of that work is hosting many social events to engage the students, faculty, administration, and community to facilitate each of these levels' understanding and appreciation of the others.

4. Description of Steps Taken to Evaluate and Improve Administrative Skills

Participated in the American Council on Education Conference for Department Chairs in Washington DC, 1995. This was extremely helpful because it was in my first year of administration, and I was able to get a very good understanding of the responsibilities and challenges I was taking on. I used the information gained there immediately and still retain a quote that I heard and keep it stored in my memory: "Give a man a fish; feed him for a day. Teach a man to fish; feed him for a lifetime."

I attend the National Association of Schools of Art and Design annually. We are accredited by this association. Through the organization, I have engaged the help of a facilitator, Robert Milnes from San Jose State University, to participate in a retreat that I held for my faculty, spring 2000 at the O'Neil House in Akron, Ohio. The purpose of this retreat was to rectify differences of opinion pertaining to the content of our foundations program. I also bring back many issues in the field to share with my faculty from these conferences. Often they are national trends or problems in schools of art.

I attend the College Art Association conference annually. At this meeting, I mainly recruit new faculty members to our school and promote our excellence. I also have had the opportunity to watch many of my faculty members give presentations at this conference and learn a great deal about them by watching them present to their peers. New information about the quality of other art schools is gained as I interview the many individuals at this conference.

I attended and presented at the International Council of Fine Art Deans. From my attendance at this conference, I established many international opportunities for my faculty. Faculty have presented workshops in Spain and Finland and given presentations in New Zealand, Finland, and Italy. We have also begun to establish a student exchange program with the University of Barcelona and a faculty exchange program in Milan.

This conference has made me more aware of curricular differences at art schools outside of the United States. My upcoming sabbatical is to look closer at the possibility of a public art program for our school, which is uncommon in the United States but not in Europe.

5. Evidence of Impact on Areas of Responsibility

We are a named endowed school because of my relationship with a long-time friend of the university. This endowment has enabled us to establish one of the best undergraduate art programs in the country. Our programming has brought enrichment to the school, the university, and to the community. This has also influenced our reputation nationally.

I have forged many strong relationships with other arts organizations, patrons, corporations, and the upper administration. These relationships have created many opportunities for the faculty and students. Among them we now have:

- A major scholarship program that includes tuition scholarships, travel scholarships, and materials scholarships

- An endowed scholarship from American Greetings for graphic design students

- A major artist-in-residency program that brings internationally known artists to the school for residencies that can range from one week to a year

- Excellent funding for faculty research and travel

I was the catalyst for a collaboration between Dale Chihuly, the world-renowned glass artist, and the College of Polymer Science that will result in a 60-foot sculpture by Chihuly in polymers. I am working on:

1) A residency that would enable our students to go to India to work with the prestigious designer Michael Aram

2) A summer program for underprivileged teens and high school art teachers through the new art ed program that we are establishing. This is also an endowed program established from a recent gift to the school.

6. Five Most Significant Administrative Accomplishments

Raising the endowment to be a named school. We are one of a few named art schools in the country. We share this great name with our patron, Mary Schiller Myers, an alumna who is well known and highly regarded throughout the art world as an advocate and patron of the arts. Mrs. Myers has served on boards and committees of many arts organizations, including the Metropolitan Museum of Art, the Whitney Art Museum, and the Cleveland Museum of Art.

Improving the quality of the school. We have completely revamped the foundations program, which is the first set of courses students take. This is where we set the standards to ensure quality and success. Our new funding has also enabled us to recruit higher quality students through our scholarship program and retain many fine students through the wonderful programs and opportunities that we offer.

Establishing the artist residency program. This program is very beneficial to our students, faculty, and the community. Working side by side with such prestigious artists has been inspirational to all of us. Engaging in their creative process by learning about their philosophies and methods has been an exceptional experience for the school. It also gives the students hands-on experience of working with artists outside of academia. Part of this program also requires that the artist give a significant work of art to our permanent collection. This collection is becoming very impressive.

Improving the atmosphere physically and enhancing the image of the school. Every visual detail is important because we are in the visual business. It is important that our surroundings exemplify this. Although there have been few funds from the university to improve our space, I raised the funds from a donor to improve the atrium space. We added new flooring and new track lighting. These improvements have enabled the students to use this space as exhibition space. I have also had many new cases built around the school, as it is crucial that we exhibit the work of our students.

I refurbished a classroom to create a faculty meeting space. We have all our faculty meetings there, and many faculty often schedule committee meetings in this space as well. We have computers in this room for adjunct faculty and/or staff use, and have faculty artwork displayed in this area.

We produced a full-color brochure that has been extremely beneficial to recruitment (see Appendix A). The design work was done by a designer from the Arocom Marketing Group. The cost of this publication would have been over $70,000, but I was able to get the CEO of the Arocom Group to donate all of the design work, and I negotiated a discounted price for the paper and printing. I recently had two of our graphic design faculty members design a new logo for the school (see Appendix B). We now have an identity system that so that all publications have the Myers look (see Appendix C).

I put together a team of students led by a faculty member to create the first web site for the school, and since have reformatted the design to be more consistent with our identity (www.uakron.edu/art/). This is proving to be a great recruitment tool for students and faculty. We constantly get compliments on the quality of the design of this site.

Improving the morale of faculty. I believe all of the above accomplishments have raised the morale of the faculty. They are very proud of the school in which they teach. Their commitment and contributions to making it a wonderful school is a strong indication of the morale of the faculty.

7. Evaluation and Performance

Select sentences from the last dean, faculty, staff, and student reviews of the director (see Appendix D, E, and F for complete reviews).

Dean's review. "At the conclusion of the faculty review, through secret ballot the faculty voted on recommending reappointment by a tally of 19 yes, 0 no, and no abstentions. Such uncontested unanimity is rare at any time."

Faculty reviews. "A review of her accomplishments shows that she has increased the morale of the faculty, increased the endowment, and increased creative, scholarly, and professional opportunities for both faculty and students."

"The school has gained a distinct measure of both credibility and respect as a result of her stewardship."

"Ms. DePaul's self-confidence and intelligence give her the strength to stand up for her beliefs and to tackle difficult situations."

"Christina has managed to maintain a high level of production in her creative work despite her responsibilities as director. Her professional reputation as an artist brings recognition to the School of Art and the university."

"Her vision, energy, creativity, and focus have encouraged faculty to be more ambitious and productive with their own creative work and their service to the school."

Staff reviews. "They feel that she has excellent communication skills, that she keeps them 'in the loop,' that she is pleasant whenever they discuss something with her, and that she is approachable when they have a situation or problem."

"They are especially appreciative of the way the school has improved and 'risen to a higher level' under her direction."

Student reviews. "The students were very familiar with Ms. DePaul and spoke well of her. The first comment was that she is 'awesome.'"

"One student mentioned that Christina is so well respected in the arts community that 'things happen' for the students that were not possible before her tenure."

8. Colleagues' Assessment of My Contributions to the School, University, and Community

(See Appendix G.) Letters from faculty, dean, president, provost, director of art museums, dean of polymer science, students, donors, development officer.

9. Continuing Contributions to the Field

I am a practicing professional artist, and constantly produce, exhibit, and/or create large-scale commissions (see Appendix H). I lecture about my work throughout the world and present at many conferences (see Appendix I). I attend art exhibitions, conferences, and read about art and design, academic art issues, and the culture that we serve.

10. Administrative Goals: Short Term and Long Term

Within the next six months, my goals are to:

- Hire six new faculty members.

- Develop a better mentoring system within the school for new faculty.

- Develop the new Art Education program.

- Work with the gallery director, gallery committee, and planning committee to raise the caliber of exhibitions in the Emily Davis Gallery.

- Facilitate the Dale Chihuly sculpture.

- Create a five-year plan for all equipment and technology needs in the school.

- Begin a new body of work.

Within the next two years, my goals are to:

- Identify funds for an addition to the building for faculty and advanced student studio space.

- Prepare for the National Association of Schools of Art and Design site visit for accreditation.

- Create a think tank for the collaboration of artists and scientists.

- Research a graduate degree program or a certificate program in materials research in polymers for artists and designers.

- Research academic programs in public art.

11. Appendices

A. School brochure

B. School identity system

C. School publications

D. Dean's review of director

E. Faculty review of director

F. Student/Staff review of director

G. Letters

H. Images of work

I. ICFAD and ELIA conference brochures

Christina DePaul is Director, Myers School of Art, University of Akron.

ADMINISTRATIVE PORTFOLIO
William K. Guegold
Director
School of Music
The University of Akron
College of Fine and Applied Arts
June 2001

Table of Contents
1. Introduction
2. Statement of Administrative Responsibilities
3. Statement of Administrative Philosophy
4. Administrative Methods, Strategies, Objectives
5. Multisource Performance Evaluation Data
6. Self-Evaluation
7. Assessment Actions for Improvement
8. Administrative Accomplishments and Evidence of Impact
9. Contributions to Administrative Science
10. Documentation of Administrative Development Activities
11. Administrative Goals: Short Term and Long Term
12. Appendices

Introduction
The purpose of this portfolio is twofold: first, to examine and evaluate what I have done, and what I currently do, as the director of the school of music; and second, to set personal goals related to my administrative responsibilities. The portfolio provides concrete narrative concerning my administrative duties, accomplishments, and goals as well as actual evidence of those accomplishments in the appropriate appendices.

Statement of Administrative Responsibilities
I am the chief academic and managerial officer of The University of Akron School of Music. The school has 31 full-time and roughly 55 part-time faculty members. We have 55 graduate teaching/research (performing) assistants, 250 undergraduate majors, and another 100 part-time graduate students. The majority of the full-time graduate students are music performance majors while the bulk of the part-timers are pursuing degrees in music education. Our undergraduate student body is about 66% music education majors with the rest falling into the performance, music history, jazz, composition, and Bachelor of Arts programs.

We have 5.5 FTE staff members (secretaries, an audio technician, and a piano repair person/tuner). The school is housed in Guzzetta Hall, with rehearsal and office space, teaching studios, practice modules, classrooms, and a 225-seat recital hall.

As director of the school, I am responsible for the unit, not only as a manager, but also as an academic leader. As such, I hire and retire faculty members, oversee the budget of the unit, serve as an ad hoc member of all school committees, supervise revision and maintenance of the curriculum, advise students, and serve as our chief human public relations front. The following table indicates the approximate time devoted to these duties:

Director's Duties

Personnel Management	50%
Financial Management	25%
Meeting and Functions	10%
Public Relations	10%
Advising/Teaching/Other	5%

The school is one of seven within the College of Fine and Applied Arts. The University of Akron has a student body of over 20,000 students and is located within the culturally diverse and rich region of northeast Ohio.

Statement of Administrative Philosophy

The title of administrator is not viewed by all as one of distinction. Those of us who hold that title can take some solace that in 1 Corinthians 12 "those with gifts of administration" are listed along with apostles, teachers, workers of miracles, prophets, among others! It's a good group to which one can be compared.

I believe it is the primary role of the school administrator to act as a facilitator for the faculty, staff, and students within the unit. Every action of the school director should have at its heart the best interests of the unit. Teachers must be free to teach. Performers must be free to perform. The staff must be free to assist. And, of course, students must be free to learn. If the administrator is an effective leader, all of these things can take place in an atmosphere of mutual respect and cooperation. In some instances, the less that the administrator is perceived as being needed, the better they have been at accomplishing their tasks.

The administrator must also be able to act as an advocate for the unit within the university community as well as within the broader spectral span outside the university. At times this may entail speaking with upper-level administrators in person or just being articulate, efficient, and timely in preparing reports that find their way into these people's hands. It also includes being visible and available to the public, who may or may not know of the reputation of the unit and university.

The academic chair cannot be everything to everyone. Yet she/he must be able to sustain a focused effort, permit faculty autonomy when appropriate, construct an atmosphere for the creation of knowledge, work alone or in a group effectively, and be an expert at customer service.

As the administrative head of the unit, it is the school director's responsibility to focus the vision of the school but not necessarily formulate that vision. Developing a unit's vision must be a group task, with input from everyone. I see the director as a leader among equals with her/his piece of the total puzzle being the last one in place, finishing the completion of the big picture.

I have always believed that the education profession is one of service to humanity. As an educational administrator, I have, and will continue to strive to take the term *service* to the highest level of my ability.

My philosophy describes why I do what I do. Putting it simply, I firmly believe it is the role of the administrator to find the best means possible for the faculty and unit as a whole to do what they do best: teach, create, perform, serve, and learn.

Administrative Methods, Strategies, Objectives
None of the above responsibilities can be accomplished alone. Including the staff listed above (who all answer directly to me), I have formed a director's advisory committee that is made up of the assistant director of the school (1/4 load), coordinator of graduate studies (1/4 load), coordinator of undergraduate studies (1/6 load), applied area chair (1/4 load), music technology coordinator (full-time), and music advisor (part-time faculty member). I delegate specific administrative responsibilities to members of this committee as appropriate.

Many of the administrative decisions of the unit are done in committee. Full faculty meetings are more informational than action oriented unless specific and extraordinary circumstances warrant (note sample faculty agenda in Appendix A). I meet informally with faculty members one-on-one on a regular basis and permit both spontaneous and scheduled appointments in an open door policy.

All school committees and the music staff (with the director and assistant director) meet monthly or as needed (in the case of curriculum and search committees). Promotion and tenure committees meet only in the fall as does the school travel committee. Regular faculty meetings are held to a strict agenda provided at least a week in advance and minutes are in the hands of the faculty, in most cases, within a week of the previous month's meeting. I also publish a monthly (or as needed) *Friendly Reminder* (Appendix A) for the faculty and staff to keep them abreast of important items concerning the school and university community. In my three and one-half years as school director, I have never called an additional meeting of the faculty outside those regularly scheduled.

School of Music
Administrative Structure

Director

Music Staff

DAC	Assistant Director	Committees
Graduate Coordinator		Curriculum
Undergraduate Coordinator		Travel
Applied Area Chair		Promotion and Tenure
Music Technology Coordinator		Searches
Academic Music Advisor		Music Teacher Ed
		Scholarship (ad hoc)
		Financial Planning
		Endowed Concert Series

All Full and Part Faculty

Students!

Multisource Performance Evaluation Data

As set in the *Bylaws of the College of Fine and Applied Arts*, school directors are to be evaluated three times by the school's faculty. The first two evaluations are informal and take place during the director's first two years of a four-year term. The third evaluation is a formal one which takes place during the forth year. This formal evaluation leads to the faculty taking action on the director's reappointment for an additional term. The actual decision is consummated in a vote of the full-time, tenure-track faculty in which the director must receive a majority of favorable votes cast to be retained for an additional term. These evaluations are to include input from the school's staff, part-time faculty, and students. Comments from these reviews included:

" . . . has good people skills."

" . . . a very decent, honest, likeable person who behaves on a reliably high scale."

" . . . a friendly, open person who makes a good impression."

" . . . knows school programs and procedures well."

"I feel very comfortable with his leadership." (staff comment)

Although my interactions with students are minimal compared to those with faculty and staff, in a survey completed by two of the major conducted ensembles, 75% of the students rated me as "adequate to good" corresponding to 6 or better on a 10 point scale.

In addition to the evaluations completed by the faculty review committee, the dean of the college supplies the director with comments accompanying the informal review during the first two years as well as a yearly review for merit pay considerations. Samples of these evaluations can be found in Appendix B.

Results of all of the various evaluations have been quite supportive. I have received positive merit recommendations from the deans in each of my three years. Although my faculty evaluations were also positive, there were several suggestions for improvement, as could be expected with such a large and diverse faculty. Faculty comments included a call for a more structured budgetary process, perhaps more freedom to dialog during faculty meetings, and a desire for the director to attend more concerts and recitals. Copies of the last three reviews can be found in Appendix C.

Self-Evaluation

Before being assigned the position of school director by Dean Linda Moore in 1997, I evaluated the school situation and came to the conclusions listed in the section on Assessment Actions for Improvement. I also assessed my own strengths and weaknesses to determine whether I was up to the challenge. My initial appointment was for two years in an interim capacity. However, at the end of the first year, the faculty voted to establish me as the regular director of the school based on my performance to that point.

At the end of each of the past three years, I have reflected on my ability to conduct the duties of the office and the strengths and weaknesses as well as needs of the school. The process included the review of our annual reports, any internal or external reviews of the department that had been completed, and the evaluations provided by the dean and faculty. Although this process has not been a formal one in any sense of the term, I have used it, along with personal conversations with faculty, staff and students, to set or reset policy and procedures for the subsequent year. In particular, these reviews have resulted in major changes in the way in which we request information from faculty concerning loads, set budgets, assign graduate assistant responsibilities, and schedule use of the music facilities.

Assessment Actions for Improvement

I inherited a faculty that was at odds, frustrated, and in many ways not functioning as a cohesive unit. Implementing a form of divide and conquer, I found that important decisions could best be made in committee and at times by director's prerogative. Sharing of information was of utmost importance and seemed to work best in written form or in personal or small group/committee settings (somewhat restricting debate). I applied a good deal of structure to the life of the school. Policies were solidified and are constantly found in the *Friendly Reminder* newsletters serving as constant reinforcement of what has been decided and what the expectations are of all faculty and students. Recognition of faculty and student successes is also touted in the newsletters and at regular meetings.

By first dividing and then conquering, I believe I have been able to bring the faculty back together as a unit that is now more functional as a whole. Faculty/faculty and faculty/staff interactions are more collegial, but not perfect. I realize there is still room for improvement and will keep working on this aspect of the position. I have attempted to tailor what I do to fit my personality and the needs of the school. Now that we have turned the corner on the unit's stability, I believe I can adapt my actions and philosophy appropriately.

Samples of the *Friendly Reminder* newsletters and many of the forms used to help direct and focus faculty requests as well as steer the director's decision-making process can be found in Appendix A.

Administrative Accomplishments and Evidence of Impact

My leadership activities are more completely documented in Appendices C and D. I have remained an active member of several campus committees and have chaired many. I was a member of the first university faculty senate and spent two years as chair of the campus facilities planning committee. I served as chair of the most recent college dean search committee. My involvement in the Ohio Music Education Association has included serving as chair and member of several important committees as well as a six-year term as president and chair of the 2000 Professional Conference held in Cleveland.

I had two main tasks upon assuming my initial appointment as interim director in 1997. The first was to bring the faculty together as a functioning unit, and the second was to prepare the school for its ten-year accrediting review (self-study, visiting team review, and final response). In each case, the tasks were successful, with the first leading to the second—our receiving a full reaccreditation from the National Association of Schools of Music.

During this period of time, we undertook a feasibility study for the addition to Guzzetta Hall. I have been instrumental in expounding the need for this increased space in many different corners since serving as chair of the Faculty Senate Facilities Planning Committee. We have been able to remodel space vacated by the School of Communications into new School of Music offices, rehearsal space for the percussion division, the construction and equipping of a new electronic music lab, and created storage, meeting, and office space for the band department. The move of communications also permitted us to include better teaching facilities for heavily loaded part-time faculty.

Giving to the school has reached an all-time high, thanks in large part to a very cooperative development office. In the past three years we have received gifts in excess of $300,000.

Contributions to Administrative Science

During my term as director of the school, we have had a 100% success rate in the formal retention, promotion, and tenure of faculty. Five professors have been promoted to full professor (Resanovic, Paolucci, Jolly, Johnston, and me). Three have been promoted to associate professor with tenure (Toliver, Davidson, and Lineburgh). We have had no negative retention decisions. And we have pending this year two promotions to full professor and six retention decisions. All of these (thus far in the process) have received positive recommendations.

During the period in which I have served as school director, we have received two grants from the Ohio Humanities Council ($1,500 each), two Dean's Faculty Research Grants ($2,000 each—Aaron and Ryon), ten faculty have been granted faculty improvement leaves (Ryon, Shanklin, Johnston, Zadrozny, Paolucci, MacGregor, Aron, Bodman, Pope, and VanderArk). Two of our professors have received summer faculty research grants (Toliver and McCarthy), two have received summer teaching fellowships (Bernstein and Toliver), and two have received university faculty research grants (Ryon, Pope). Many of our students have also received dean's student activity grants (various amounts), and our faculty and staff have performed and presented their research all over the world.

Former students whom I have advised and taught have gone on to assume leadership positions in the field include Brian Ebie (PhD at Kent State), Jack Blazey (department chair in the Painesville City schools), and Darryl Kubilis (department chair in the Highland Local schools). Letters demonstrating the impact of my administrative roles can be found in Appendix F.

Documentation of Administrative Development Activities

I have attended four of the last six National Association of Schools of Music conferences (San Francisco, Boston, Chicago, and San Diego). Sessions that I attended included those in faculty development, preparing for the self-study and visiting accreditation teams, post-tenure review, innovations in music technology, and fundraising. The most valuable of these were the two dealing with the self-study preparation (as I had not been through that process before) and post-tenure review (as I now have to evaluate tenured and promoted faculty for merit raise consideration).

I participated in the Peter Seldin teaching portfolio workshop sponsored by the College of Fine and Applied Arts during January of 2001.
As a result, I was able to refine my administrative vision and organize my
administrative persona in a clearly presentable format. The four-day
workshop included intensive writing assignments, individual and group
sessions with the facilitators, resulting with the production of a nearly
complete administrative portfolio.

Administrative Goals: Short Term and Long Term
My long-term goal is to see that as I continue to grow as an administrator and refine my management/leadership skills, the School of Music
will grow with me. The school is one of the largest music units in the
state and in the top 50 nationwide in terms of enrollment and credit-
hour production. Although we are at or near critical enrollment mass
based on budget, facilities, and faculty resources, we can increase the
quality of work performed and students recruited and graduated. Within
the next five years, I would like to see significant growth in our gradua-
tion rate at both the graduate and undergraduate levels and a substantial
increase in our undergraduate student retention rate.

Short-term goals should help achieve the long-term strength of the
unit. During each of the next three years, I would like to see us obtain
development funds increased for scholarships, create one or more
endowed faculty chairs, and a named donor for the school. We need better print and electronic media representing the true image of the unit. I
want to increase the opportunity for faculty and students/student groups
to travel. We should develop several strong concert series with the funding to bring in guest artists and clinicians on a more regular basis. It is
important for us to improve our facilities by upgrading the acoustical
treatment of the building and working for an addition to Guzzetta Hall
that is functional and allows us to expand our current programs. I believe
I can contribute to a continuation of an upbeat faculty morale, coupled
with strengthening the reputation of the school both within and outside
the university community.

Appendices

A. Faculty Meeting Agenda/ *Friendly Reminder* Newsletters/ Forms

B. Faculty Evaluations

C. Dean's Evaluations

D. Administrative Accomplishments (OMEA Program, Annual Report, NASM Review Comments)

E. Committee Chair List

F. Letters of Support

William K. Guegold is Director, School of Music, University of Akron.

186   *The Administrative Portfolio*

ADMINISTRATIVE PORTOFOLIO
Laurence D. Kaptain
Assistant Provost-Academic Affairs
University of Missouri, Kansas City (UMKC)
Administrative Portfolio
June 1, 2000–May 31, 2001

Table of Contents

Introduction
Steve Ballard, Vice-Provost of Graduate Studies at Bowling Green State University, will assume the position of provost and vice chancellor for academic affairs at the University of Missouri, Kansas City on July 1, 2001. The primary purpose of this portfolio is to appraise him of the evolution of the job of assistant provost, from June 1, 2000 to May 31, 2001. It will also provide a framework to evaluate my job performance, and explore the possibility of further defining this position.

Why would I leave a career as a successful teacher in the UMKC Conservatory of Music? What sense does it make to cut back on an international concert career of live performances, broadcasts, and recordings? The simple answer is that a different chord has been struck—one that resonates in the deepest parts of my intellect and spirit. I have not given up on music—I have changed instruments. Instead of playing percussion, I'm inventing new possibilities for others and myself. These possibilities are exciting and very tangible.

Today I am involved in projects that are both facilitative and central to the mission of the university. I want to show through this portfolio that I am preparing to be a leader of organizational and curricular transformation and change in higher education at the local and national levels. This leadership will result in improved student learning outcomes through community engagement.

Institutional context. In preparing our community of learners for the challenge of the 21st century, UMKC has almost 13,000 students enrolled in distinctive undergraduate programs, graduate and professional studies, and an innovative Interdisciplinary PhD program. There are three areas of eminence that have been identified as central to UMKC's distinctiveness as a metropolitan university:

1) Visual and performing arts

2) Health sciences

3) Urban affairs (academic programs such as law, business, and education, which are important to urban communities)

With programs and services related to its mission as a metropolitan, land-grant university, the university serves the greater metropolitan area, the state of Missouri, and beyond through the provision of quality education, engagement in research and scholarship that extend the boundaries of knowledge, and service as an active community partner in the economic, educational, and cultural development of the region.

The Blueprint for the Future

Under the leadership of Chancellor Martha W. Gilliland, UMKC is engaged in a process of organizational transformation which is being facilitated by Gordon Starr of Starr Consulting. Over 1,600 stakeholders have participated in this dynamic process, in which three principal themes have been identified thus far:

1) A Campus without Borders

2) Academic Excellence: Building on our Strengths, Nurturing Innovation

3) An Environment that Unleashes Human Potential

The Blueprint for the Future is a commitment to UMKC becoming a university that is the catalyst for transforming higher education. As Chancellor Gilliland said in her inauguration on September 29, 2000: "These times call for new standards of excellence in higher education. A few universities will have the courage to respond to the times and define the new. UMKC will be one of those. UMKC will respond by defining the new standards for higher education."

Administrative Responsibilities: The Office of Academic Affairs
Academic affairs is where my office and accountabilities lie. This unit does not function within a vacuum. The best results are obtained when the scholarly and creative energy of UMKC is complemented by programs in student life and the other structural units. My current duties include being theme leader for the Blueprint project; leading undergraduate curriculum and programs/general education; New Faculty Teaching Initiatives—UM System; Liaison: registrar, Information Technology Advisory Council, financial aid, admissions, student life/student affairs, commencement, university catalog; champion—TLT Roundtable; facilitator for assessment/COPE reviews; faculty development; International Academic programs; director of university Center for Interdisciplinary Studies at UMKC; founder and publisher of monthly newsletters *Teyolcuitiani*—supporting the transition from faculty teaching to student learning, and *Scholars for a New Century*—faculty roles and rewards; establishing learning communities at Twin Oaks (UMKC's planned residential site for living and learning); pre-med undergraduate screening for Arts and Sciences/School of Biological Sciences; facilitator/coordinator of new Coordinating Board of Higher Education Transfer and Articulation Procedures; UMKC representative to Kansas City Missouri School District HEP (Higher Education Partnership); staff member/coordinator of Conservatory Dean's Search.

Here is a breakdown of my perception of the time I spend:

• 20% Blueprint theme leader and Blueprint activities/meetings

• 20% Facilitative matters assigned by the provost

• 20% Meeting attendance, academic affairs representation/response

• 15% UM system matters/initiatives

• 15% Faculty matters

- 10% Community engagement

I will speak to some of the major initiatives in which I am involved:

- The programs and policies of my administrative responsibilities provide many challenges. There is a broad diversity of content and structure that require a tandem of intellectual understanding and aptitude as well as leadership and facilitative skills.

- My greatest challenge is being the interim theme leader for the Blueprint Project: A Community of Learners. Chancellor Gilliland has presented me with a tremendous opportunity, but also a huge responsibility. In recent days, she has requested that I work with Gordon Starr, of Starr Consulting, to produce a leadership development plan, and she has also charged me in this capacity with becoming a great leader. I take that challenge seriously and am putting considerable energy toward that journey.

- Undergraduate curriculum and programs/general education are being developed further to equal the infrastructure that has been achieved already for graduate education. I have suggested to the chancellor that leading undergraduate education at UMKC should be someone's full-time job.

- As co-founder of the University of Missouri New Faculty Teaching Scholars, I have helped contribute to a system-wide program that will also have discrete elements within each campus. I have learned a great deal from interacting extensively with both UM system officers and campus faculty and administrators. This has provided me with a broader perspective of what potentials lie ahead of the University of Missouri.

- Establishing learning communities at Twin Oaks and across the campus is another challenge that requires an understanding of the core values of UMKC as an institution. It also presents an opportunity to draw on the intellectual capital of the metropolitan area.

- Faculty development has afforded me the most personal satisfaction, as there has been no centralized faculty development program at UMKC. Bringing the national dialog of best practices to this campus has been extremely satisfying, yet daunting, as there is no established center on this campus.

- Overseeing a new International Academic Programs Office has been an example of staying out of the way of something special. Director Daniel Stoll has done a wonderful job in a short amount of time in establishing his office as a student, faculty, staff, and community resource.

- There has been a continued dialog on interdisciplinary studies at UMKC. More faculty need to invest their time on it, and administrators need to make the tough decisions. Next year will be spent in hearing from the very best curricular planers of interdisciplinary studies so that UMKC may have a program that embeds itself into the institution, rather than standing alone.

- One of the first things I did after joining academic affairs was to publish two monthly newsletters. Many faculty and staff have expressed enthusiasm for reading about the transition from faculty teaching to student learning— *Teyolcuitiani*—and another on faculty roles and rewards—*Scholars for a New Century*.

- Historian Stephen Ambrose gave a major address at UMKC that provided a clarion call for A Community of Learners: Transformation in Higher Education Conference. As leader of the process to identify and select 40 Meriwether Lewis fellows and 20 Corps of Discovery members, I view the Community of Learners: Transformation in Higher Education Conference as a tipping point in the evolution of UMKC to a world-class institution.

Reflective Statement

I work daily with a multi-billion-dollar budget of intellectual and cultural capital, both at the university and within the community. It is with that perspective that I share the following:

Philosophy. I am a lifelong learner. Enthusiasm for learning has been a constant in my life, and something I am eager to share with others. This provided a good fit with the interim provost who hired me— Marjorie Smelstor, who served UMKC from June 1999 through December 2000. She and the second interim provost, Bill Eddy, both brought a strong sense of civic engagement and public work to their philosophical base of the university's role. I could not help but be influenced by their examples. My own views have been further shaped by Mary Walshok who has headed up the inspirational programs of community engagement in LaJolla at the University of California, San

Diego. Her writings stress the need for universities to embrace civic knowledge and not necessarily view themselves as the sole or primary source of knowledge within the community. That has influenced me in the way I view the community—as a resource, not as a group standing with its hand out.

I stand for the possibility that student learning outcomes need to take precedence over process. In that regard, students learn much more by doing and being engaged in active learning, than by passively listening to lectures. Experiential learning, problem-based learning, learning outside the classroom are all at the heart of my philosophy of education—education made to measure, as the president of Columbia University Teacher's College, Arthur Levine states. He recently wrote, "We need a new vision of education—one that recognizes the unique way every student learns." That expresses my own feelings, and what I believe we are able to accomplish at UMKC.

In addition, I'm always both moved and inspired by Harry Boyte, senior fellow and co-director of the Center for Democracy and Citizenship at the Hubert H. Humphrey Center, University of Minnesota, who believes that civic engagement needs to be addressed with a rigor and recognition that lies within the academy's promotion and tenure/roles and rewards policies. I live with that image every day and try to imbue those principles within my work and contact with colleagues.

My own definition of the word *stakeholder* within higher education is broad. I view the institution's work as being something that ties in with public work and the issues that reveal the crucial elements of civic culture.

Objectives. My own objectives are global. I will continue to increase my level of efficiency, as well as continue to present at and attend conferences, make site visits, and review the media surrounding the national dialog in higher education. I feel that my analytical skills and perceptions can be put to good use in turning new strategies and best practices into going past the doable and into the terrain of transformational initiatives at UMKC.

Strategies. The strategy that I bring to this position is one of primary focus on outcomes. While process can certainly contribute to the end result, I put the balance of my energy into doing whatever it takes to find the end result. To that end, I endeavor to inspire others through focusing on their own strengths and showing them how enrollment in a particular project can bring them personal benefit.

Methodology. My primary focus is to treat people well. When walking into the office every day, I carry that concern with me. The next focus is to carry out my responsibilities in a timely manner. This requires a great deal of multitasking. Until recently, I did not have any direct clerical/facilitative support and therefore had difficulty in maintaining the efficiency the job requires. This situation has now changed for the better.

This personal methodology is perhaps best explained in qualitative research terms. Ronald J. Chenail, editor of the *Qualitative Report,* speaks of the seven C's: curiosity, confirmation, comparison, changing, collaborating, critiquing, and combinations. Those words express the range of methodologies I employ.

- Curiosity led me to leave my musical career for the challenges of higher education transformation, leadership, and administration.

- Confirmation is something I do daily with my colleagues at all levels, both on campus and at institutions across the nation.

- Comparison is one way that we may gauge our progress, that is by looking at Indiana University–Purdue University, Indianapolis, George Mason University, and other institutions on a similar journey.

- Changing is what the Blueprint is all about.

- Collaborating is something I have done my whole life as a musician.

- Critiquing is something I do to my own work every day.

- Combinations reflect the multitasking this job takes.

I would add creativity as a methodology, as I'm constantly searching for new ways to engage our faculty. Faced with doing many things the same way (and extending the way their professors did them), faculty welcome creative ways of approaching the new scholarships of discovery, teaching, integration, and engagement.

And finally, these Nauhatl (Aztec) words guide my actions in my job as Assistant Provost:

- Student: momachtiani—Literally: one who causes/enables himself/herself to know/ learn

- Teacher: teyolcuitiani—Literally: one who causes/enables others to give direction to their potential

- Education: neyolmelahualiztli—Literally: process of giving direction to people's potential

Multi-Source Performance Evaluation Data

I asked faculty, administrators, and community stakeholders for evaluations on both upward and downward aspects of my job performance. As I expected, several evaluators commented on the potential for growth they see in my work. There is a great deal that I have learned from this. Not only does it reflect on the perceived alignment of performance outcomes to the job description, but also it provides a mirror of what others view as the most important dimensions of this position. Appendix A includes original letters from all of the individuals who are quoted below.

- Dean of the UMKC Dental School Michael Reed said, "I believe Larry continues to be challenged by his roles of assistant provost, academic affairs and has displayed the characteristics necessary to meet these challenges."

- It was heartening to learn that members of the faculty recognize that the number of tasks in my job description grow almost daily. Chair of the UMKC history department Patrick Peebles said, "...I am in awe of his ability to carry on what he calls *multitasking* with extraordinary energy and good cheer. That he has done this while working under interim provosts in a situation where the university has little experience with active provosts is all the more remarkable."

- The health sciences are removed both physically and discipline-wise from my career as a teacher, scholar, and musician. Patricia Marken, Chair of the UMKC School of Pharmacy, "...Dr. Kaptain is committed to a new model of defining achievement at UMKC, and when he becomes committed to an idea he sticks with it. 'Strong and credible leadership is crucial during this time of transforming UMKC into a world-class institution,' to quote the chancellor."

- A major personal thrust that I bring to my work is an interest in working in and with the city. Growing up in a diverse and ethnically rich area of Chicagoland, I always lamented the distance that people of distinct cultural and socioeconomic backgrounds make for themselves. National Organizer of Public Achievement (based at the Center for Citizenship and Democracy of the Hubert H. Humphrey Institute at the University of Minnesota) Dennis Donovan noted, "I have found Larry to be very thoughtful and accountable. Larry is very serious about wanting to make a difference. He demonstrates this by his leadership, people skills, and work ethic. He knows how to get things accomplished."

- Blueprint Breakthrough Project leader and American Dental Education Faculty Fellow John Killip reports to me in his capacity as a Breakthrough Project leader in the PRIDE (UMKC roles and rewards group), and stated, "Larry brings to this position an endless energy and excitement for the university within the sphere of higher education in America. All the while he remains humble and sees his place as facilitating the future rather than forcing his vision on members of our campus community."

Administrative Innovations and an Assessment of Effectiveness
The office of the provost in academic affairs has become empowered to take a campus-wide leadership role to promote academic excellence. Everything we do is new and sets a new standard that needs to be evaluated for effectiveness. Along with the Blueprint process, we have identified a cadre of talented faculty across the campus who are working together to transform UMKC.

Success at this point? That's difficult for me to say. Perhaps the performance evaluation letters shed light on the direction in which things are headed.

Efforts to Improve/Develop performance
Select books read and referenced

- Damrosch, David. *We Scholars.*
- Boyer, Ernest. *Scholarship Reconsidered.*
- Zohar, Danah. *Rewiring the Corporate Brain.*
- Biancolli, Amy. *Fritz Kreisler.*
- Collins and Porras. *Built to Last.*
- Gladwell, Malcolm. *The Tipping Point.*
- Bolman, Lee. *Leading with Soul.*

- Light, Richard. *Making the Most of College.*
- Lencioni, Patrick. *The 5 Temptations of a CEO* and *Obsessions of an Extraordinary Executive.*
- Walshok, Mary. *Knowledge without Boundaries: What America's Research Universities Can Do for the Economy, the Workplace, and the Community.*

David Damrosch's book, *We Scholars,* provides a framework and context for Boyer's sweeping and influential work *Scholarship Reconsidered.* On a different level, Danah Zohar, *Rewiring the Corporate Brain,* applies concepts of quantum and chaos thinking to the working world, utilizing spiritual, mental, emotional, stimuli all working for transformation and positive change. This has been an excellent model for me in the Blueprint process we are engaged in at UMKC. In Amy Biancolli's biography of violinist Fritz Kriesler, I learned about another type of transformation—that of the unleashing of the human spirit through music without words. That provides a paradigm of providing leadership in higher education that relies on the potential that lies within each person.

It would be a mistake to define Collins's and Porras's seminal work *Built to Last* as a book about businesses. It's a book about people and unleashing their human spirit. In *The Tipping Point,* Gladwell sustains and imbues that notion of human contact and the language of a few can change the world. Lee Bolman's book *Leading with Soul* reinforces this—treat people well and empower them to change, then step back.

Richard Light's recent book about what college students think extends Mary Walshok's premise of looking beyond the traditional structures of universities as the sole source of learning and intellectual capital and assets.

Select national/international workshops/conferences attended from June 1, 2000 to May 31, 2001

- **Asheville Conference on General Education** (AAC&U): Laurence Kaptain led a five-member faculty team from UMKC.
- TLT (teaching, learning and technology) **National Conference:** Laurence Kaptain led a four-member faculty team from UMKC.
- **Salzburg Seminar No. 382 Civic Responsibility and Youth:** Models of Participation AGLS (Association of General and Liberal Studies): Laurence Kaptain made presentation (see Appendix B).

- **AAHE** (American Association for Higher Education) **Roles and Rewards:** Laurence Kaptain led a 12-member faculty team from UMKC to the AAHE National Conference.

- **AAHE National Conference:** Laurence Kaptain made a presentation (see Appendix B).

Application of what was learned. The lessons I learned at these conferences have added many dimensions to my pedagogical, methodological, strategic, and philosophical base. Perhaps the most visible outcomes from these conferences are the two newsletters that I founded and publish, *Teyolcuitiani* and *Scholars for a New Century.* The most important forum for sharing my ideas has been the Blueprint activities in which I am involved.

An unexpected and most welcomed outcome of this conference attendance and interactivity, has been the formation of a core of mentors. I have regular contact with Deborah DeZure, Coordinator of Faculty Programs at the Center for Research in Teaching and Learning at the University of Michigan; Marilyn M. Leach, Director, Center for Faculty Development The University of Nebraska, Omaha; Thomas Lowe, Dean of the University College at Ball State University; James Groccia, Director, Program for Excellence in Teaching and Special Assistant to the Dean of the Graduate School (University of Missouri, Columbia); Devorah Lieberman, Vice Provost and Special Assistant to the President, Campus Initiatives, and Director, Teaching and Learning, Portland State University.

Evidence of Impact on Areas of Responsibility (See Letters of appreciation, Appendix B.)

Five Most Significant Accomplishments

1) Published two monthly newsletters beginning in July 2000: *Teyolcuitiani* and *Scholars for a New Century* (see Appendices C and D).

   - This has helped create a network of conversations regarding the national dialog in higher education and potential applications to this work of transforming UMKC.

2) Established Assistant/Associate Deans Council, February 2001.

   - The assistant and associate deans at UMKC literally run the day-to-day business. By convening this group, there is greater communication surrounding issues of admissions, retention, continuing education, applications of technology to learning and teaching, and many other issues.

3) Established a reconfigured Blueprint Undergraduate Council for Excellence, May 2001.

- While this is still in the process of formation, it will provide a viable means for moving undergraduate education up to the level of support that graduate programs currently enjoy.

4) Established a two-day conference on transformation in higher education May 14–15, 2001. Led the selection/identification of 40 Meriwether Lewis faculty fellows and a 20-member Corps of Discovery.

- Drawing inspiration from the heroic expedition of explorers Lewis and Clark, UMKC produced a two-day development workshop on issues surrounding faculty roles and rewards and civic engagement through living and learning. The outcomes of this endeavor will propel the efforts of the Blueprint Theme Group: A Community of Learners. In the broadest terms, this conference developed leadership at UMKC to support the development of living and learning programs (support the Blueprint Model Campus Living group); renewal of civic responsibility; diversity at UMKC on social, political, economic, and academic levels with an inclusive multicultural curriculum; defining faculty roles in the scholarships of teaching, integration, and engagement (support Blueprint PRIDE group on changing faculty roles and rewards).

5) Initiated Fulbright Conference, hosted by the office of international academic programs on April 23, 2001.

- This conference was hosted by the Office of International Academic Programs and brought in a guest facilitator from the Fulbright Office in Washington, DC—Carol Robles. Aside from the workshops she presented, a reception was held for all Fulbright recipients at institutions of higher education in the Greater Kansas City area.

Administrative Awards/Recognition (See Appendix E)
  Fulbright Study Abroad grant. (June 2001), administered by the
U.S. Department of Education.

- 15 university presidents'/chancellors', provosts', and deans' tour
  of leading institutions of higher education in Brazil to encourage
  exchanges/consortia and linkages with US institutions.

Hispanic Heritage Society Special Recognition Award. (September
16, 2000)

- One of two Special Recognition Awards presented at Fiesta His-
  pana by Kansas City's largest Latino cultural organization: "For
  initiating a working relationship between the Greater Kansas
  City Hispanic Heritage Committee, Inc. and UMKC and for
  providing and teaching the wonderful rhythmic sounds of the
  marimba and maintaining an exchange program with Chiapas,
  Mexico."

Thomas Barr Fellowship. (September 2000)

- Awarded a full fellowship to attend the Salzburg Seminar #382,
  Youth and Civic Participation: Models of Engagement. Fifty-
  nine fellows were selected from 39 countries. Laurence Kaptain
  later convened a presentation at the AAHE national conference
  of two participants from the Salzburg Seminar (Cericie Olatunji
  of Xavier University of Louisiana, and Karen Scates, CEO of
  Kid's Voting USA).

Contributions to Conferences/Journals/Books

- Association of Graduate and Liberal Studies (AGLS) conference, An
  Integrative Resource: The Resident Ethnic Music Ensemble.
  Chicago, November 2000.

- American Association for Higher Education (AAHE) national conference. Collaborations between K-16 Non-profit Organizations
  and Colleges and Universities. Washington, March, 2001.

- Julius Wechter. A discography, bibliography, and biography. *Percus-
  sive Notes,* Vol. 39, No. 1. February, 2001, pp. 53-62.

  Creative activity—featured performing artist

  - Twentieth Century Unlimited-Santa Fe (June 2000)

- Release of Stravinsky recording by New York Orpheus Ensemble (July 2000)
- Edmonton Symphony Orchestra (September 2000)
- Charleston Symphony Orchestra (October 2000)
- Southeast Iowa Symphony Orchestra (October 2000)
- Chicago Symphony Orchestra (four concerts in Orchestra Hall, international syndicated broadcast, January 2001)
- Sospeso Ensemble in New York's Lincoln Center with composer Pierre Boulez (March 2001)
- Eos Orchestra in New York City (two concerts and proposed CD recording in May 2001)
- Residency at Arizona State University (April 2001)
- New York Philharmonic—five concerts in Lincoln Center (April 2001)

Creative Activity—administrator

- Co-artistic director of Stravinsky Festival—a collaboration of The Kansas City Symphony, the Kansas City Ballet, The Lyric Opera of Kansas City, and the UMKC Conservatory of Music. January–March 2001.

Community Activity
Because of my scholarly/creative accomplishments in the music of Latin America, I have been honored to serve numerous organizations that represent Latino cultural interests in the Greater Kansas City area. My fluency in Spanish and many travels throughout the Americas have given me credibility that has helped UMKC sustain and improve community relations (see Appendix E).

- Sociedad Hidalgo—Board of Directors (Kansas City-based Latino cultural organization)
- Compassion Foundation—Board of Directors (Kansas City-based foundation to improve education and social conditions of children in the maquilladora district of Ciudad Juarez)
- Pembroke Hill School Arts Council

- Member, Economic Development Committee for Jackson County—Arts and Culture Subcommittee

- Grupo Atotonilco—Board of Directors (Kansas City-based Mexican folkloric dance troupe)

- Hispanic Showcase Benefit Concert—Planning Committee, June 15, 2001

- COMBAT 3rd Annual Poetry Contest—Planning Committee for May 5, 2001—hosted by UMKC (sponsored by the Jackson County Prosecutor's Office).

Administrative Goals: Short and Long Term

Short-term goals. (June 1, 2001–May 31, 2002)

- Assist the new provost in establishing his base of academic/programmatic leadership.

- Continue to demonstrate leadership for the Blueprint.

- Convene the new Blueprint Undergraduate Council for Excellence to map, guide, and lead the direction of undergraduate education at UMKC.

- Develop interdisciplinarity in the curriculum and new learning communities.

- Support director of international academic programs on increasing UMKC faculty applications and acceptance of Fulbright awards.

- Establish New Missouri Teaching Scholars program, a UMKC/UM System Faculty Development Program.

- Establish a community of learners monthly faculty development conference to support the broadening of scholarly activity at UMKC.

Long-term goal. (June 1, 2001–May 31, 2006)

- Fulfill Chancellor Gilliland's challenge to become a great leader. From my perspective, that would be a leader of organizational and curricular transformation and change in higher education at the local and national levels.

Appendices

A. Statements from Others

B. Conferences/Presentations

C. Newsletters/Articles

D. Programs

E. Awards/Community Involvement

Laurence D. Kaptain is Assistant Provost, Academic Affairs, University of Missouri, Kansas City.

ADMINISTRATIVE PORTFOLIO
G. Roger Sell
Director
Center for the Enhancement of Teaching
University of Northern Iowa
Cedar Falls, IA
April 2001

Table of Contents

J. Faculty and Administrator Unsolicited Comments on the Impact of the QEP Project

K. Follow-Up Evaluation of the May 2000 Humanities Institute

L. Unsolicited Comments on the Impact of Center Director Contributions to the Chilean Educational Reform Project

M. Provost's Letter of Commendation for Contributions to the NCA Self-Study and Accreditation Process

N. Faculty and Administrator Unsolicited Comments on the Impact of the Center's Organizational Development Activities

O. Comments on the Center Director's Impact on the Scholarship of Teaching

P. 1998 Alumni Survey

Q. Student Views of General Education

R. Faculty Views of General Education

S. Reviewer Comments on "Using Technology and Distance Instruction to Improve Postsecondary Education"

T. Description of Robert J. Menges Award

U. External Reviewer Comments on the Impact of the Center Director on the Practice of Professional and Organizational Development

V. External Reviewer and UNI Faculty Comments on the Overall Effectiveness of the Center Director

W. Some Recent Contributions to Books, Journals, External Research Projects, and Conference Sessions

Introduction

When I began preparing this portfolio, my intention was to document my performance for a summative self-evaluation. However, I found that development of this portfolio challenged me to reflect deeply on what makes me tick, how I view my professional work and my institution, the availability and interpretation of evidence about my performance, and where and how I can improve. This portfolio, then, serves both a formative and summative evaluation of my role as director of the Center for the Enhancement of Teaching at the University of Northern Iowa.

Institutional context. The University of Northern Iowa (UNI) is a public comprehensive university that has a history and mission distinct from those of the other colleges and universities in Iowa. Over its 125 years, the University of Northern Iowa evolved from a normal school to a state teachers college, a state college, and a state university. The university's faculty and academic programs are organized in the departments of five colleges (Business Administration, Education, Humanities and Fine Arts, Natural Sciences, and Social and Behavioral Sciences), each headed by a dean who reports to the provost and vice president for academic affairs. UNI enrolled (headcount) 12,218 undergraduate students and 1,556 graduate students in fall 2000, and employed approximately 600 tenured and pre-tenure faculty and 300 adjunct faculty.

Organizational unit context. The Center for the Enhancement of Teaching (CET) was implemented in spring 1993. The center's mission is to engage UNI faculty by supporting them in their individual and collective efforts to improve teaching and learning throughout the university. The center's advisory committee, which issues an annual report to the Faculty Senate, consists of one representative of each the five colleges (elected), the library (elected), and the Faculty Senate (appointed by the chairperson). An associate provost serves as an ex officio committee member. In addition to the director, the center's staff includes a half-time instructional consultant, faculty fellows who receive stipends or release time for center projects, and secretarial support. The current budget for the center totals approximately $250,000.

Administrative Responsibilities
When interviewing for the center director's position, it became clear that expectations for the center and the director's responsibilities varied widely. Consequently, I began by conducting an extensive, five-month needs assessment study to involve faculty and academic administrators in setting the center's agenda and defining more fully the primary responsibilities of the director. The following ten goals for the center emerged and frame the current responsibilities of the director (not listed in any order of priority):

1) Serve as a university-wide resource, information clearinghouse, network, advocate, and/or catalyst for teaching.

2) Support faculty in their individual and collective efforts to improve teaching and learning.

3) Help to improve the evaluation of teaching and its recognition and reward.

4) Provide programs for all faculty that help them in their continuing development and renewal as teachers.

5) Assist in incorporating technology into teaching and learning, and collaborate with support services to eliminate barriers for instructional innovation.

6) Promote a broad and balanced view of scholarship that gives attention to the importance of teaching as well as research and service.

7) Work with faculty and student services to address issues of student preparation, expectations, and development.

8) Focus on general education, class sizes, and related concerns for improving the undergraduate experience.

9) Encourage and support research on teaching and learning.

10) Work with faculty and academic administrators to develop an environment that nurtures and rewards effective teaching and that is sensitive to ethnic, gender, and social diversity.

These ten center goals and the needs assessment from which they emerged are discussed in "Building a University-Wide Center for Teaching and Learning: A Preliminary Report" (Appendix A) and illustrated through the framework of center goals and activities found in Appendix B.

Statement of Administrative Philosophy

Some of the values and beliefs that are part of my personal philosophy include:

- Treat each person with respect and dignity.

- Expect that each person can be successful with appropriate challenges and support.

- Experience life as a process of becoming and unfolding, where change and development are regularities rather than exceptions.

- Value the diversity of life in all of its forms and expressions, with the whole being more than the sum of its parts.

- Be open to new possibilities for improving our individual and collective lives.

- Connect with others and work collaboratively to address common problems and to accomplish mutual aspirations toward a society that practices freedom for all.

In carrying out my administrative responsibilities, these personal beliefs and values are challenged by at least two competing imperatives: 1) balancing the relative emphasis on maintenance and improvement activities and 2) responding to the needs and expectations of multiple constituencies.

From my perspective, university administration involves management, planning, and leadership not only for maintaining the organization but also for improving it. Maintenance is required if the university and its members are to have the necessary human, financial, physical, and information resources to function day to day. However, maintenance is not sufficient for a vital, healthy organization or the well-being of its members (students, faculty, staff, administrators). Without attention to improvement, organizations and individuals atrophy—they become uncritical, ineffective, or even dysfunctional.

Because higher education institutions serve several internal and external constituencies with different needs and expectations, conflicts also exist regarding the goals, resources, activities, and outcomes that should receive priority. For me, the essence of university administration is located in defining and resolving complex (often unstructured) problems in an environment characterized by dialectical tensions, such as respecting and appreciating diversity while striving for common purpose and unity; creating freedom for individual initiative and expression while developing commitments to community and civic responsibility, promoting change for development and improvement while creating a trusting and supportive environment that provides dependability and stability, encouraging and practicing inquiry and reflection while making decisions and taking action, and focusing on development strategies while attending to the impact of evaluation and reward systems on perceptions and performance. Administering a teaching center involves almost daily problem solving and creativity with regard to these conflicts and dialectical tensions.

Administrative Strategies and Objectives

My major responsibilities include development work of various kinds. Development implies improvement, and improvement requires change. While not all change results in improvement, improvement in policies and practices is not possible without learning (individually and collectively) for deliberate, purposeful change. Within this orientation, much of what I do involves the design, implementation, and evaluation of development strategies that engage faculty and administrators in learning to change (improve) with regard to themselves, their students, the curriculum, their organization, and external audiences.

Specific change strategies focusing on different kinds of development—faculty development, curriculum development, and organizational development—are reflected in the following examples of goal-oriented activities carried out under my leadership:

- Orientation, mentoring, and follow-up for all new tenure-track faculty (and faculty colleagues who serve as mentors of new faculty)

- Individual consultations involving classroom observations, in-class interviews, student evaluation of teaching instruments, self-evaluations

- Workshops, seminars, and institutes designed to actively engage faculty in professional development

- Individual and group projects aimed at the understanding and improvement of learning, teaching, courses, the curriculum, and/or the university as an organization

- A university-wide conference for bringing faculty together with staff, administrators, and students to explore a topic or theme of importance to the functioning and improvement of the institution as a whole

- A website, professional newsletters, occasional papers, journals, books, and other materials that support effective teaching and learning

- Research aimed at broadening and deepening the understanding of learning and teaching, courses and the curriculum, the role of technology, and how faculty and academic administrators have an impact on the quality of university life

- Professional involvement beyond the university to discover new perspectives and resources, to learn from other practitioners and institutions, and to provide opportunities for university faculty and academic administrators to share their work (and contributions of the institution) with others

These change strategies are embedded below in the evaluation of my leadership for the center.

Performance Evaluation: Multi-Source Evidence of Impact

To what extent, and supported by which evidence, do I provide effective leadership in fulfilling the ten goals established for the Center for the Enhancement of Teaching? Multiple sources of information are used to answer this question, including:

- Institutional records of the center and the university (see Appendix C for the number of faculty who participate in center activities and Appendix D for faculty participation rates in center activities for randomly selected departments)

- Questionnaires, surveys, and interviews of those who participate in center activities (See Appendix E for a follow-up study of new faculty and their mentors and Appendix K for a follow-up study of a center institute.)

- Unsolicited faculty and administrator evaluations of the center (See Appendices F, H, I, J, N, and O for faculty and administrator comments on the center's seminars for senior faculty, instructional consultations, professional development activities, Qualities of an Educated Person project, organizational development activities, and scholarship of teaching activities.)

- External reviews of the center director's performance (See Appendices L, S, U, and V for external reviewer comments on the center director's contributions to an international education project, center publications, the field of professional and organizational development, and overall effectiveness.)

- Awards and recognition received by the center (See Appendix M for a letter of commendation from the university provost and Appendix T for the description of a recent professional award.)

These sources of evaluative information are woven into a critique of my leadership of the center with regard to impact on 1) faculty development, 2) course and curriculum development, 3) organizational development, 4) the scholarship of teaching and learning, and 5) the larger profession of professional and organizational development in higher education.

Impact on faculty development. Two center goals focus on faculty development: Provide programs for all faculty that help them in their continuing development and renewal as teachers, and support faculty in their individual and collective efforts to improve teaching and learning throughout the university. To accomplish these goals, I provide leadership for the orientation and mentoring for new faculty, seminars designed for faculty at various career stages, and instructional consultation. The complete study of the spring 2000 follow-up with new faculty and their mentors is found in Appendix E.

- **Faculty seminars.** One of the standard features of teaching centers is a series of faculty seminars or workshops. In consultation with faculty and administrators, I designed our seminar series at UNI to help meet the needs of faculty with different interests and at different career stages. For example, new (pre-tenure) faculty seminars include topics such as: facilitating discussion in classrooms, improving your course design, assessing and grading your students' learning, and balancing teaching and research. The center experiments with a variety of seminars for tenured faculty, including ones designed specifically for the renewal of teaching. The significant and positive outcomes of an experimental seminar with senior faculty are indicated in the participant comments found in Appendix F. Approximately one-half of the current UNI faculty have participated in one or more center seminars.

- **Instructional consultation.** Approximately 25% of the current UNI faculty can be described as occasional or regular users of the center's in-class interview or Small Group Instructional Diagnosis (SGID) technique. Based on faculty self-reports and independent empirical evidence, these SGID-aided consultations frequently have the following beneficial effects:

  - Systematic inquiry into and reflection by the faculty member on his/her teaching, the course, and the learning of students

  - Identification of similarities and differences among students in their responses to the course and the instructor

  - Diagnosis of student responses in locating and explaining potential changes that could be made to improve the course and the students' learning experiences

  - Development of the faculty member's teaching knowledge and skills

  - Improved end-of-course student ratings of teacher effectiveness

Examples of unsolicited comments and empirical evidence to support these claims about the impact of instructional consultations using SGIDs are found in Appendix H.

Impact on course and curriculum development. Center leadership for course and curriculum development (or instructional development) includes several large-scale projects such as the Qualities of an Educated Person (QEP) and its experimental sub-projects, the Humanities Institute, technology initiatives in collaboration with professional staff from Information Technology Services (ITS), and the Fifty-Seven Fund.

- **Qualities of an Educated Person (QEP) project.** The first university-wide conference sponsored by the center uncovered this question: Which qualities do we wish our graduating students to possess? The center became the organizational home for faculty who created their vision of the purposes of an undergraduate education and the student qualities consistent with that vision. Experimental projects for developing and assessing the proposed qualities were funded through the center with financial support from the provost. Comments that highlight the impact of the overall QEP project are found in the faculty and administrator comments in Appendix J.

- **Humanities Institute and follow-up consultation.** For the first time since the present General Education program was adopted in 1986, faculty who teach humanities courses are supported with stipends (equivalent to research grants) for an extended institute (the first one was in May 2000) and follow-up instructional consultation (the first ones were in fall 2000) aimed at enhancing student learning and satisfaction in general education. Nine faculty who participated in the first institute. Follow-up faculty interviews documenting professional development and instructional changes resulting from the Institute are reported in Appendix K.

- **Technology applications for teaching and learning.** The Humanities Institute is one key venue for exploring and developing new technology applications for teaching and learning in general education courses. Also in collaboration with the Division of Educational Technology, I am spearheading UNI's involvement in MERLOT, a consortium involving 23 systems of institutions that are developing a library of peer-reviewed, web-based, multimedia materials and associated learning experiences for higher education applications.

- **The Fifty-Seven Fund.** Originating with a gift from the Class of 1957, the center offers faculty small grants (up to $250) to involve UNI alumni in their courses. For the first two years (1998–2000) of the '57 Fund, UNI faculty submitted proposals and received support for bringing 49 alumni to campus to interact with undergraduate students in their classes.

Impact on organizational development. Center leadership for organizational development focuses on three goals: 1) Serve as a university-wide resource, information clearinghouse, network, advocate, and/or catalyst for teaching; 2) help to improve the evaluation of teaching and its recognition and reward; and 3) work with faculty and academic administrators to continue to develop an environment that nurtures and rewards effective teaching and that is sensitive to ethnic, gender, and social diversity. Current center activities contributing to organizational development include faculty networking; an annual conference for bringing faculty together with staff, students, and administrators around a topic of importance to the quality of the university; development of student evaluation of teaching instruments; contributions to university diversity initiatives; and contributions to institutional assessment such as the NCA self-study for accreditation and UNI strategic planning.

- **Faculty networking.** Center events and programs draw on faculty across the university as planners, organizers, facilitators, presenters, evaluators, and participants. In support of faculty collaboration and networking, the center provides electronic (website) and logistical (space and materials) support to help faculty connect with one another on an almost daily basis.

- **University-wide conferences.** Each year the center sponsors a university-wide conference around a topic or theme selected for interest to faculty as well as staff, students, and administrators. Often, faculty bring their classes to conference sessions. This annual conference grew rapidly from 175 participants in 1995 to nearly 1,000 participants in 1998. Parker J. Palmer, a national leader in college teaching, presented a series of seminars in fall 2000 and a public convocation open to the general public. In addition to university participants, conferees included teachers and administrators from the surrounding public schools.

- **Evaluation of teaching.** A Student Assessment Review Committee (SARC), which I facilitated developed a new student evaluation of teaching form and reporting system for the university. The SARC endorsed my recommendation to provide faculty with improved formative evaluation support in order to obtain feedback for instructional improvement, including diagnostic student evaluation forms, minute papers, the SGID process, and systematic classroom observations.

- **Diversity initiatives.** In support of the university's diversity's goals, work with the Center for Multicultural Education and support external consultants and speakers during Diversity Week on campus; serve on a student retention committee; host several breakfasts and other occasions for minority faculty pursuing tenure; participate in the multicultural education seminars for faculty sponsored by the Department of Educational Psychology and Foundations; sponsor a seminar series featuring international faculty; design university conference sessions each year with diversity as one of the themes; and work with the Office of International Programs to engage faculty and academic administrators in activities associated with international education week. I also serve as a workshop leader and consultant for the democratic educational reforms in Chile, whose project director made the unsolicited comments found in Appendix L.

- **NCA self-study for reaccreditation.** I took part in the three-member UNI Coordinating Committee for the North Central Association (NCA) self-study and reaccreditation process. A provost's letter of commendation for this contributions is found in Appendix M.

Impact on scholarship of teaching and learning. Center leadership for the scholarship of teaching and learning focuses on two goals: 1) Promote a broad and balanced view of scholarship that gives attention to the importance of teaching as well as research and service, and 2) encourage and support research on teaching and learning in the university. Current center activities contributing to a scholarship of teaching and learning include a model for faculty portfolios; inquiry associated with Small Group Instructional Diagnosis (SGID) activities; experimental studies undertaken through the QEP project; and reviews of research literature on teaching, learning, and technology.

- **Faculty portfolios.** I worked with one department to create a policy statement for faculty portfolios and a model for how scholarship in faculty activities (teaching, research, and service) can be documented and evaluated with portfolios. The use and impact of these faculty portfolio practices are addressed in the comments found in Appendix O.

- **SGID inquiry.** As noted above, the SGID technique has been used widely at UNI to gather and use formative feedback from students for understanding and improving courses while they are in progress. A first-order concern in establishing a scholarship of teaching and learning is to attract faculty interest in generating good questions for inquiry. The SGID process is designed to evoke questions about teaching and learning in a specific course and, therefore, is a bedrock form of the scholarship of teaching and learning at UNI.

- **QEP experimental studies and surveys.** Many of the experimental efforts supported through the QEP project contribute to the scholarship of teaching and learning. QEP assessment activities also include a survey of four cohorts of alumni (a project co-sponsored by the center), the report of which is found in Appendix P, and a survey of current students enrolled in two sections of a general education course, the report of which is found in Appendix Q. From another perspective, Appendix R analyzes views of general education from a UNI faculty survey and what can be done to strengthen general education. These initial inquiries establish baseline data.

- **Reviews of research literature.** Three of my recent reviews of research literature are useful for framing questions and designing assessment studies regarding 1) conditions and practices for assuring quality courses and programs offered through distance learning, 2) what we know about learning with technology and how we know it, and 3) the effectiveness of faculty workshops based on 29 published research studies.

Impact on the larger profession. Beyond UNI, my leadership in the field of professional and organizational development occurs in several ways: research and development sessions offered at the annual conference of the Professional and Organizational Development (POD) Network in Higher Education, organizing and governing activities of the

POD Network, member of journal review boards, and contributor to publications.

- **POD conference sessions.** Each year, four to eight UNI faculty conduct research for and offer sessions at the POD annual conference. Along with two other UNI faculty, the director is a first-year recipient of one of three POD Honored Presentation Awards in Recognition of Robert J. Menges, which is described in Appendix T.

- **POD leadership.** Beginning spring 2001, I will serve as president-elect for the POD Network. Recent contributions include governance activities on the POD Core Committee (1997–2000) and conference chair for the 1998 POD Conference.

- **Journal review boards.** I also currently serve as a member of the *Peer Review* and Knowledge Network advisory boards of the Association of American Colleges and Universities (AACU) and a member of the editorial board of the *Journal of Innovative Higher Education.*

- **Publications and conference presentations.** Appendix W includes a partial list of my recent contributions to books, journals, external research projects, and conference sessions. The themes across these research and creative activities reflect my primary work in professional and organizational development: faculty development and evaluation; curriculum development, instructional development, and technology; organizational development and assessment; and research strategies for disciplined inquiry in education.

Five Most Significant Administrative Accomplishments
Major recent accomplishments associated with my center leadership are:

- Developing the SGID process for instructional improvement, for faculty professional development, and for inquiry at the bedrock level in contributing to a scholarship of teaching and learning

- Designing the Qualities of an Educated Person (QEP) project for explicating knowledge, skills, and values expected of UNI graduates as educated persons and translating these qualities into curricular and co-curricular models for use by individual faculty, faculty teams, curriculum committees, academic units, and academic support units

- Negotiating agreements among a committee representing faculty, administrators, and students for the creation of an innovative student evaluation of teaching form and reporting system
- Establishing systematic studies of student, faculty, and alumni views of general education as a framework for using assessment to improve the undergraduate curriculum
- Contributing to the leadership of professional and organizational development as a field of reflective professional practice in higher education

Administrative Goals: Short-Term and Long-Term Intended Accomplishments

Short-term administrative goals. For the next year or two, my administrative goals are to:

- Extend innovative uses of the SGID process to more faculty through collaborative faculty teams who conduct in-class interviews and serve as consultants for one another.
- Design, offer, and evaluate a revised Humanities Institute and a new capstone workshop, both of which are aimed at improving student learning and satisfaction in general education courses.
- Collaborate with the Center for Multicultural Education in offering campus diversity workshops.
- Offer evaluation of teaching workshops for department heads and faculty chairs of Professional Assessment Committees.

Long-term administrative goals. Over the next five years, my administrative goals are to:

- Establish a well-supported program for encouraging and developing department heads in their role as faculty developers and faculty mentors in their role as instructional consultants.
- Upscale the Humanities Institute and capstone workshop into an ongoing General Education Institute in collaboration with the Educational Technology Division of ITS and Educational and Student Services.
- Promote diversity in all facets of the university—campus population, institutional policies, undergraduate and graduate curriculum

and co-curriculum, and teaching and learning practices—in working with university constituencies, administrative offices, and external audiences.

- Establish the Center for the Enhancement of Teaching as a national leader among comprehensive universities in the practice of assessment and the scholarship of teaching and learning.

- Work with the Core Committee, executive team, and organization membership to increase the visibility and effectiveness of the POD Network in Higher Education.

Appendices

A. "Building a University-Wide Center for Teaching and Learning: A Preliminary Report." Cedar Falls, IA: Center for the Enhancement of Teaching, June 1993

B. A Framework Portraying the Goals and Activities of the Center for the Enhancement of Teaching

C. Number of Faculty Participating in Center Activities Annually over a Six-Year Period (1994-1999)

D. Faculty Participation Rates in Center Activities over a Six-Year Period For Randomly Selected Departments of the Five UNI Undergraduate Colleges

E. Follow-Up Study of New UNI Faculty and Their Mentors (Spring 2000)

F. Unsolicited Faculty Comments on the Impact of the Center's Senior Faculty Seminars

G. A Plan for Senior Faculty Development

H. Unsolicited Faculty and Administrator Comments on the Impact of Instructional Consultations Using the In-Class Interview (SGID)

I. Faculty and Administrator Unsolicited Comments on the Impact of the Center's Faculty Professional Development Activities

J. Faculty and Administrator Unsolicited Comments on the Impact of the QEP Project

K. Follow-Up Evaluation of the May 2000 Humanities Institute

L. Unsolicited Comments on the Impact of Center Director Contributions to the Chilean Educational Reform Project

M. Provost's Letter of Commendation for Contributions to the NCA Self-Study and Accreditation Process

N. Faculty and Administrator Unsolicited Comments on the Impact of the Center's Organizational Development Activities

O. Comments on the Center Director's Impact on the Scholarship of Teaching

P. 1998 Alumni Survey

Q. Student Views of General Education

R. Faculty Views of General Education

S. Reviewer Comments on "Using Technology and Distance Instruction to Improve Postsecondary Education"

T. Description of Robert J. Menges Award

U. External Reviewer Comments on the Impact of the Center Director on the Practice of Professional and Organizational Development

V. External Reviewer and UNI Faculty Comments on the Overall Effectiveness of the Center Director

W. Some Recent Contributions to Books, Journals, External Research Projects, and Conference Sessions

G. Roger Sell is Director, Center for Enhancement of Teaching, University of Northern Iowa.

ADMINISTRATIVE PORTFOLIO
Joan North
Dean
College of Professional Studies
University of Wisconsin, Stevens Point
Spring 2001

Table of Contents

1. Introduction
2. Context
3. My Values and Operating Style
4. Previous Goals and Accomplishments
5. Reflections and New Goals
6. Appendices
   A. Focus on teaching evidence
      Results of 1999 and 2000 CPS staff surveys on the impact of the college focus on teaching
      List of upgraded classrooms and college dollars committed
      The CPS teaching/learning web site
      The college's application for the University of Wisconsin System Teaching Excellence Award
      List of scholarly work on teaching/learning by CPS faculty
      List of CPS Teaching Partners by year
      Annotated bibliography of works on teaching/learning in the CPS library and from which books are bought for faculty
      My article on the need for deans to support teaching
      Marty Loy's article "When a College Supports Teaching"
   B. Quality of work life/culture of civility evidence
      Statements from all CPS department heads
      Pictures of physical changes in buildings
      List of time management changes department heads and me
   C. Development evidence
      List of gifts for past year
      List and pictures of special events and visits to donors
      Copy of specially designed cards for thanks, events, invitations, and Thanksgiving
      Pictures of flower arrangements I made for donors
   D. Reflective practice evidence
      List of my publications/presentations for past three years

List of books and articles I have found stimulating
E. WWHEL evidence
New state website
State conference brochures for past three years
List of UWSP women attending last three state WWHEL con-
ferences
Recommendations from UWSP Forum on Women in Adminis-
tration
List of women hired for recent UWSP administrative positions
F. Results of 1998 University-Wide Joan North Supplemental
Review

Introduction

Who knows if all the Yogi Berra quotes are truly his, but I think "You can see a lot by observing" could be the theme for this portfolio. In the past five years, I have become quite committed to reflective practice in my administrative work. Developing a portfolio is one natural outcome from thinking and talking about one's work.

Purpose and audience? I envision this portfolio serving both developmental and evaluation purposes. I plan to use it as the centerpiece of my annual evaluation with the vice chancellor and to share it with my department chairs and several professional friends for their feedback. Since I am five to seven years from retirement, I also see this document as a capstone experience, capturing my best and final years.

Context

The College of Professional Studies (CPS) at University of Wisconsin, Stevens Point (UWSP) houses 11 undergraduate majors and four Master's programs in six CPS schools/divisions: School of Education; School of Health; Exercise Science and Athletics; School of Health Promotion and Human Development; School of Communicative Disorders; Division of Interior Architecture; and Programs in Medical Technology and Military Science. We represent a diverse group of pre-professional programs, about 1/3 of UWSP's 8000 enrollment, including the majority of graduate students. Pre-professional programs are characterized by profession-driven curricula, national testing for students, close collaboration with professionals, and long-term, supervised internships. I have served as dean for 15 years.

As dean of a loose federation of semi-independent schools/divisions/programs, my role differs greatly from that of a dean of a more focused college, such as a college of education or a college of fine arts, especially since there are no professional staff assigned to my office. This context helps to solve the usual dilemma over concentrating on management tasks or soaring to leadership challenges. I have neither the staff nor the discipline-specific intimacy to overdose on close management tasks.

Nonetheless, in flipping through my calendar for the year I find 31 personnel decisions, 43 interviews with prospective faculty, 105 regular meetings with the department heads individually and as a group (CPS Cabinet), and multiple meetings with the Faculty Senate, Graduate Council, Board of Visitors, Foundation Board, Athletics Committee, Teacher Education Committee, Foundation Allocation Committee, and On Advancement Group. Since I am the campus teacher certification officer, I also examine and sign around 400 teacher certifications a year and work with others on various K-12 projects: beginning teacher, accelerated certification, integrated teacher education data base, technology grants, new state license rules, and enrollment caps.

Each year brings its own special opportunities/problems: a new major, lab/classroom upgrades, tours for new board members, athletics' opportunities, and personnel issues. This year I also attended/presented at meetings or conferences in Chicago (twice), Vancouver, Madison, Oshkosh, San Francisco, Milwaukee, and Wisconsin Dells. Banquets, luncheons, picnics abound. I play tennis twice a week and I keep my commitment to ring the Salvation Army bells in the snow at the University Center at Christmas.

My Values and Operating Style

Be yourself. A major influence on how I operate is my mother. When my mother died in 1990, one year after she retired from a miserable work life, I vowed to walk a different path. We spend the vast majority of our time in work settings; if our work is unfulfilling or straining, then we are exhausted and empty the vast majority of our time on earth. For me, the new path led directly to liberating the real me and letting it loose in my work settings. While we all adopt personas on various occasions, the inclination to act like an administrator is strong every day, especially among women and minorities who have seen few administrators like themselves. This disconnect between who you are supposed to be and who you really *are* can cause both personal discomfort and professional flops from the strain of keeping the mask up. When more of my inner self is sitting at my desk, I smile more, act less formal, think forgiveness over justice, eschew competition, and sometimes perform random acts of kindness. I guess the inner me is more of a person and less like a title. In addition to my mother, I credit Parker Palmer's book *The Courage to Teach* (1998), in which he challenges teachers in classroom settings to teach from their inner selves, without which connections with both what you do (content) and with whom you work (students or colleagues) are impossible.

Servant-leadership. A bit of honesty from my inner self helped reveal that my job had been too much about my own performance. Am I a good dean? Am I handling this conflict well? Do I represent the college well? Am I getting my share of resources? What do people think of me? Feeling that the spotlight was directed at me on the hot seat, I could become impatient, unreasonable, depressed, fearful, or too separated from the very people who make up the college. Eventually, I came to appreciate the concepts of servant-leadership, thinking about my job more as contribution to others, contribution to the department heads, to the faculty, to the university. How can I help? How can I help remove barriers from others? How can I help with their work? How can their accomplishments beam in bright lights? Administration is not about how well administrators do, but about how well the faculty, staff, and students do and, ultimately, how the collective does. As I thought about how this might apply in a teaching situation, I thought of the servant-leader type being like the guide on the side versus the sage on the stage. The servant-leader (guide-on-the-side) facilitates the group's success, rather than spotlighting his/her own performance. While this approach may sound wimpy, let me observe that it is far more difficult to assist a group of individuals toward goals than simply to shine on one's own.

Inherent in servant-leadership is a developmental bent toward helping others achieve their goals, while at the same time attempting to advance collective causes. Advancing the collective agenda within a servant-leadership context is not simply being responsive to the group. Rather, it is an action-oriented approach, made more effective by the leader's ability to hear the group and articulate a clear collective image.

Foster development. I also used to think that an administrator's job was to make change happen, to get people to do things. This administrative imperative can be frustrating and misleading because it suggests that forward-looking ideas reside with the administrators who must convince or cajole the faculty who are either clueless or stubbornly recalcitrant. Who would want to be on either side of that tug-of-war?

Actually, individual and groups of faculty almost always have dreams and challenges of their own, even if they are not especially motivated to achieve other people's agendas. Redefining my role from change agent to facilitator of growth/evolution changed the locus of control and freed others to do their good work. Using support instead of push, I began to feel less like a traditional boss and more like a jungle guide hired to chop a path through the bureaucratic jungle, enabling people to get where they wanted to go. I often envision the story about Mahatma Ghandi: One day he was sitting talking with friends. He suddenly stood up and said, "I have to go now. There go my people, and I am their leader."

So, fostering opportunities supplanted making change happen. Searching for the thread of opportunity promotes optimism, mental health, and positive outcomes. Opportunity has us looking for the learning moment or for the way to make a difference or for the secret to making a curmudgeon laugh. Opportunity has us look outside ourselves—to our students and our community—so that we are part of larger constellations. Opportunity transforms us all to active, reflective learners. Opportunity not only suggests finding new sources of funding or ways to meet new needs; it also fosters creativity in matching people with tasks. And chasing opportunity is much more fun than concentrating on control or mandating change.

I want to confess that at this point in my life, I love being an administrator; I love the work I do and the people with whom I share leadership.

Previous Goals and Accomplishments

An administrator has so many routine responsibilities and unanticipated problems that it is both difficult to find time for goals and necessary if you want to accomplish anything outside the normal menu.

Focus on teaching. Reflecting on how deans can get distracted from explicitly supporting teaching, I came to believe that focusing on teaching did not come naturally in the job and required an explicit commitment. About nine years ago, the college unit heads and I announced our goals to make teaching more visible in the college and to facilitate more open discussion about teaching among all staff. In 1999 and 2000, electronic surveys of college staff reaffirmed their desire that we continue the CPS focus on teaching. Respondents noted a positive effect on their teaching and on their students' learning and pride in the physical appearance of CPS classrooms. See Appendix A or http://cps.uwsp.edu/survey/ teachlearn/1999/SurvStat.asp and http://cps.uwsp.edu/survey/teachlearn/2000/Results.asp for the results.

Our college's focus on teaching has produced a new group of ten faculty/staff teaching partners each year, resulting in an almost 90% participation among the teaching staff in the college. Since I attend their meetings, I get first-hand impressions about the challenging issues with which teaching staff struggle.

We also continued our efforts to upgrade classrooms with both college and outside funds. Over a seven-year period, the CPS chose to use about $200,000 of college funds for upgrades, resulting in improvements in every classroom in the college. We will continue with technology upgrades but are more than halfway there. See Appendix A or www.uwsp.edu/CPS/Facilities/Classroom.

Recently we created a teaching-learning library in which there are now over 100 books and periodicals. The number of items checked out for each of the past three years have been 42, 27, 48. In addition, for the past three years we have offered to buy one book on teaching, from an annotated bibliography, for any CPS staff member. Over 70 staff participated last year. We created a website which links to many excellent programs across the country and highlights the CPS focus on teaching programs. See Appendix A or http://www.uwsp.edu/CPS/Academics/TeachLearn. We also amended our travel policy to include support for one person per unit to attend a teaching conference. Finally, when we created a new college position for instructional technology two years ago, we made working with faculty to integrate technology into classrooms its highest priority.

UWSP nominated our college for the University of Wisconsin System Regents' Teaching Excellence Award in February; we will know if we won by May. A copy of the proposal is at the college focus on teaching web site listed above. The complete application is in Appendix A.

My most significant event this year was being awarded the Pierleoni Spirit of POD Award in Vancouver this fall at the annual Professional and Organizational Development Network (POD) Conference. This most special award from the national organization of professionals in faculty development crowned my efforts to make teaching our focus.

Quality of work life/culture of civility. After a series of unpleasant situations in several units, the unit heads and I devoted a summer retreat to the issue of if and how chairs have influence on the way department members treat each other and on how our general physical environment boosts us or drags us down. So often, departments simply accept abusive behavior or unpleasant surroundings because they see no options. We grappled with the differences between academic freedom and group expectations of each other and between seeking more positive behavior and seeking dismissal. The unit heads examined ways to create a greater culture of civility in their units which would promote more collegiality and make work life more pleasant. Some approaches included a yearly catch-up meeting between each faculty member and the department head, a conflict management workshop for students and faculty, and off-campus retreats.

As a byproduct of these discussions, we broadened our efforts to find new ways to improve the quality of work life in the college. We found more work time by cutting down the number of our meetings, and we added student help.

Looking to the physical aspects of our work life, we have improved office chairs, added scent machines to bathrooms, painted stairways in bright colors, painted dark hallways, added schedule holders for classrooms and offices, used leftover carpet tiles for offices, offered staff full-spectrum light bulbs, planted flowers around the building, provided pizza one day when the cafeteria was closed, and replaced hallway ceiling tiles. While these changes did not alter personalities, they did contribute to a culture of caring about the college, each other, and our surroundings. Coming to work in our building seems more pleasant. And wonderfully, magically, our work seems to gain creativity, excitement, and optimism. Of course, that is just my impression.

College connections and development. With state support of our university dipping down to 38% of our operating costs, it was probably inevitable that the four college deans would enter the field of development. In December 1999 we hired our first development officer for the college who helped us articulate our goals of deepening our connections with our supporters and raising more funds for both program support and scholarships. This new thrust takes up about 30% of my time, so it has been a struggle to shoehorn this new priority into my full schedule. Nonetheless, I have been pleasantly surprised by both how personally rewarding and how productive our efforts have been. In roughly the first year, we have identified about 100 friends of the college's programs and developed a plan for keeping in touch with them, sponsored our first former faculty fest, entertained major donors at a chancellor's garden party, established or increased almost 20 scholarships, run six separate annual campaigns which brought in about $56,000, and received over $36,000 toward endowments. Most notable are the dozens of older alums with whom we have reconnected, alums whose stories and loyalties make my day. For details, see Appendix C or www.uwsp.edu/cps/Information/CPSGiving.htm.

Reflective practice/scholarship. For the past several years I have more consciously adopted a habit of reflective practice on the events, actions, and results surrounding us. Like reflective practice with teaching, this habit of thought offers hope for understanding why we do what we do and improving the craft, as well as improving the academy through scholarship. As dean, I am sometimes challenged to explain why scholarship is important in a teaching university. I am at ease with my depictions of the differences between the practitioner and the faculty member, the latter having the luxury (and duty) to add to the profession. But when I heard Lee Shulman talk about the scholarship of teaching a few years ago, citing his dentist as an example of a reflective practitioner, I realized that there is a natural scholarship of administration as an outcome of reflective practice. And so I began to practice what I was preaching. In the past few years I have worked with the CPS cabinet and others to examine assumptions behind what we do and have shared those insights in the professional arena with four publications and ten national presentations on issues such as developmental post-tenure review, using more complex evaluation of teaching, women as administrators, using departmental meetings for cohesion, and renovating classroom spaces. See Appendix D or for a complete list, see www.uwsp.edu/cps/staff/jnorth.

Wisconsin Women in Higher Education (WWHEL). As one of the few women in an upper administrative position at UWSP, I feel compelled to encourage campus and state women to consider and prepare for future leadership positions. I have used my association with the new state organization, Wisconsin Women in Higher Education (WWHEL) and its campus affiliate to further this personal goal. At the state level, I served as a founding board member, helping with creating the mission, website, and three statewide conferences. For the past two years, I served as state co-director of WWHEL, handling communication and finances. On campus, I helped create a UWSP WWHEL steering committee; mentoring groups for new faculty; a campus-wide forum to assess campus needs (which resulted in the creation of an administrative internship among other programs); monthly breakfasts; and campus teams for the annual

WWHEL conferences. Women affiliated with WWHEL have filled almost all new positions at UWSP in recent years. Nice.

Reflections and Goals

As I begin to think about retirement, I wish I knew what others thought about when they are in viewing distance (at least with binoculars) of retirement. It does dominate the landscape. While I am not ready to start cleaning out my files, neither do I feel the pressure to build a dozen castles. Two unfinished castles are enough to fill up my days:

1) With most previous goals now ongoing, integrated into the fabric of my time and the college's life, the development castle will continue to need work, with so many alums and friends with whom I need to spend time and to match their interests with college needs. My goal for the next two years is to facilitate at least two new major endowments and to identify at least 30 additional new friends of the college.

2) The other castle is in teacher education. With major changes in state rules governing teacher education marching in through 2004, I need to spend more time facilitating our campus' ability to document our teacher education graduates' accomplishments in comparison with state standards and with extending our relationships with beginning teachers.

After 34 years in the work force, I still wake up eager to take on the day's surprises, partially because I have cultivated (fought for and trained) a habit of optimism, humor, and curiosity about the future and partially because of the high caliber of people with whom I work, especially the department heads in the college. With them, we are a team that can echo Pogo in saying "We face almost insurmountable opportunities."

Appendices

A. Focus on teaching evidence
   Results of 1999 and 2000 CPS staff surveys on the impact of the college focus on teaching
   List of upgraded classrooms and college dollars committed
   The CPS teaching/learning web site
   The college's application for the University of Wisconsin System Teaching Excellence Award
   List of scholarly work on teaching/learning by CPS faculty
   List of CPS Teaching Partners by year

Annotated bibliography of works on teaching/learning in the CPS library and from which books are bought for faculty

My article on the need for deans to support teaching

Marty Loy's article "When a College Supports Teaching"

B. Quality of work life/culture of civility evidence

Statements from all CPS department heads

Pictures of physical changes in buildings

List of time management changes for department heads and me

C. Development evidence

List of gifts for past year

List and pictures of special events and visits to donors

Copy of specially designed cards for thanks, events, invitations, and Thanksgiving

Pictures of flower arrangements I made for donors

D. Reflective practice evidence

List of my publications/ presentations for past three years

List of books and articles I have found stimulating

E. WWHEL evidence

New state website

State conference brochures for past three years

List of UWSP women attending last three state WWHEL conferences

Recommendations from UWSP Forum on Women in Administration

List of women hired for recent UWSP administrative positions

F. Results of 1998 University-Wide Joan North Supplemental Review

Joan DeGuire North is Dean, College of Professional Studies, University of Wisconsin, Stevens Point.

REFERENCES

Edgerton, R., Hutchings, P., & Quinlan, K. (1991). *The teaching portfolio: Capturing the scholarship in teaching.* Washington, DC: American Association for Higher Education.

Eble, K. (1978). *The art of administration: A guide for academic administrators.* San Francisco, CA: Jossey-Bass.

Higgerson, M. L. (1996). *Communication skills for department chairs.* Bolton, MA: Anker.

Millis, B. (1995). Shaping the reflective portfolio: A philosophical look at the mentoring role. *Journal on Excellence in College Teaching, 6*(1), 65-73.

Rodriguez-Farrar, H. B. (1995). *Teaching portfolio handbook.* Providence, RI: Center for the Advancement of College Teaching, Brown University.

Seldin, P. (1997). *The teaching portfolio: A practical guide to improved performance and promotion/tenure decisions,* (2nd ed.). Bolton, MA: Anker.

Seldin, P., & DeZure, D. (1999). *The administrative portfolio: An adaptation of the teaching portfolio.* Paper presented for the American Association for Higher Education, National Conference, Washington, DC.

Seldin, P. (2000). *The teaching portfolio.* Paper presented for the American Council on Education, Department Chair Seminar, Tampa, FL.

Seldin, P. (2001). *The administrative portfolio.* Paper presented for the American Association for Higher Education, National Conference, Washington, DC.

Shore, M. B., et al. (1986). *The teaching dossier,* (revised). Montreal: Canadian Association of University Teachers.

Smith, R. A. (1995). Creating a culture of teaching through the teaching portfolio. *Journal on Excellence in College Teaching, 6*(1), 75-99.

Zubizarreta, J. (1994, December). Teaching portfolios and the beginning teacher. *Phi Delta Kappan,* 323-326.

Zubizarreta, J. (2001). Private discussion

INDEX